JOSSINE ABRAHAMS

PEACE AFTER THE STORM

FINDING SUCCESS AFTER DOMESTIC VIOLENCE AND ABUSE

To Babette,
My dearest friend,
this will give you
the clue of my
life. Hope you will
learn something about
life.

DEAN THOMPSON PUBLICATIONS

First published in Great Britain in 2018 by Itayi Garande of
Dean Thompson Publications
An imprint of Thompson Care Limited

Copyright © Jossine Abrahams 2018

The right of Jossine Abrahams to be identified as the author
of the work has been asserted by her in accordance with
The Copyright, Designs and Patents Act 1988.

Without limiting the rights under the copyright reserved above, no part of this
publication may be reproduced, stored in, or introduced into a retrieval system,
or transmitted in any form or by any means (electronic, mechanical,
photocopying, recording, or otherwise) without prior written permission.

ISBN: 9781982992347

Contact Jossine

Telephone: +447724575725 or +442036433546 (L)
Email: peaceafterthestorm2018@gmail.com
Website: www.jossineabrahams.com
Twitter: @Jossineabrahams
Instagram: abrahamsjossine
Facebook: Jossine Abrahams
Amazon: www.amazon.com/JossineAbrahams

Contact the Editor

Itayi Garande
Email: itayig@hotmail.com or info@thompsoncare.co.uk
Telephone: +447342372234
Instagram: itayig
Facebook: Itayi Garande

WHO IS JOSSINE ABRAHAMS?

Jossine was born in Africa. She came to Britain in the early 1990s. Jossine completed healthcare studies in the United Kingdom. She now lectures in health and social care and customer services in colleges around London and the counties. In addition, she teaches individuals to write books by having seminars, webinars and group class teaching.

She is a serial entrepreneur who owns several businesses in the U.K. Jossine was first published in 2014 and since then she has published seven books. Three of the books are written solo. She also has four anthologies that she has written with other authors across the world. This book, *Peace After The Storm*, is a must-read.

The book is a very emotional recollection of Jossine's personal journey of triumph against domestic violence and physical abuse. Jossine is an award-winning author. All her books have been bestsellers. She has won several humanitarian awards for her unstinting dedication to empowering young women. As an internationally recognised inspirational speaker, Jossine says her mission is to help others to reinvent their lives after facing domestic violence and abuse.

ACKNOWLEDGEMENTS

It is an honour to acknowledge some of the most important people I value and respect who have helped a lot in building my faith and empowered me on my journey.

It is a privilege to be under their umbrella in the body of Christ. With their teaching and guidance, I had to come to terms with my life and became content with what I have. The wisdom they have invested in me is awesome. No one can take that away from me again.

Let me thank the reverends of my church, Woolworth Methodist Church in southeast London. Revs. Paul Weary and David Hardman, thank you. May God bless you all for the wonderful teaching? I would also like to thank the whole church for making me feel at home. You helped me deal with many of my challenges. To the Women's Fellowship, thank you so much for your support.

Thank you to my consultant, Dr. C. Taylor. I have confided in you at some of my most challenging moments. You have given me hope. You are always supportive and ready to assist every time I come to you. You are always ready to assist me. You have become a family member rather than my consultant. Thank you and your team for the endless support. God bless you.

I would like to thank staff at Princess Elizabeth Hospital in Essex for their amazing work. Dr. Marina Nani, thank you for listening to my story and for prompting me to speak out.

Thank you to sister Florence Bili, a corporate lawyer, for the foreword to this book. Florence, you have been a huge pillar to me. God bless you.

My editor, Itayi Garande, thank you for your patience and all the hard work you put in for this book to come through.

I also want to thank myself for having the courage to share my story with the world. I hope that some people 'riding the storm' will benefit from my experience. It is well and in Christ alone that my hope is found. He is my light, my strength and my shepherd.

I love you all.

Jossine

FOREWORD

By **Florence Bili**

Jossine Abrahams is a successful healthcare professional who owns her own healthcare business. She was born in Africa and moved to the United Kingdom with her daughter in the early 1990s. She is also the CEO of Life Change Training, Home Care Ltd and Zim-South Foods in London. Additionally, she is a part time lecturer at a FE College and teaches a health and social care course.

My first meeting with Jossine was when I was introduced to her niche retail grocery outlet on one Saturday afternoon. I left the shop energised and invigorated at warmth and inspiration of her story, particularly, how she overcame domestic violence and abuse. She struck me that she was no ordinary person, but a powerhouse who was passionate about seeing women set free from the shackles of domestic violence and abuse.

Peace After The Storm takes you through a journey of triumph and victory. Through this book, Jossine shows that you can be a victor and not a victim and that your setback is a setup for a comeback.

Candid and to the point, Jossine shares some of her lowest moments in life and demonstrates how she was able to emerge victorious through what she describes as her basement level moments. If you are looking for inspiration on how to be strong in the face of domestic violence but most importantly, how to overcome, then this is a must-read book.

Prior to penning *Peace After The Storm*, Jossine has written several books which include four anthologies and two solos. She dedicates this book to her deceased mother who was also a victim of domestic violence. Jossine wishes to encourage others that life can change. After the storm, all we need is a little faith and hope.

Jossine's books have all been best sellers and she has been nominated for the Author's Award. She has won several awards for humanity and now she has become a Coach and International Speaker for women who face abuse like her experience. In her spare time, Jossine enjoys taking long walks to the park, jogging, swimming, knitting, socialising and cooking.

Florence Bili is a United Kingdom based lawyer, educator and trainer.
(LL.B, PGDip Law, LL.M, MBA (Leadership))

WHY THIS BOOK?

This book is about my personal journey. It is about challenges of being a woman in a judgemental society. It is about society treating women like chattels, like pieces of furniture. I seek to reach out to those women who experienced struggles in society and in marriage.

Many women, young and old, suffer because they feel *rejected*. I want to encourage them that there is life after problems. They can thrive against all odds. My wish is for people to understand that if they face problems, they should not give up. Every cloud has a silver lining.

I say to women, "Do not allow situations to take over and dictate which way you go. Keep fighting until you win the battle. We have what it takes within us to come out at the other end, feeling stronger and more equipped." Humans always adjust. Just do not short-change yourself. In today's world, one has to hustle in order to survive. It is not an easy life out there.

We live in a world where we have good people and bad people. However, one has to keep their faith intact and seek their strength from their divine source. I am grateful to be able to write my third book, *Peace After The Storm*.

The process of writing this book has liberated me. It has brought healing of the wounds in my heart. Not many women want to share experiences that have brought them shame and pain. However, I will take the courage to speak of my experience today and hope to save others going through the same experiences.

As women, our beauty comes from within. I believe that a problem shared is a problem solved. Some of the most truthful and painful experiences of my marriages will touch many people. The scars of my life have resulted in me being single, maybe for the rest of my life.

I thank God for not abandoning me through thick and thin. I had to find my own way of dealing with hurt, abuse, deceit and anger. Do not be alone. We are in the same boat. Life has its vicissitudes but always remember that dreams do come true.

Jossine

This book is dedicated to my mother

who was a survivor

of domestic violence and abuse

PART 1

ONE

WHAT SCARED THE HELL OUT OF ME?

I was married three times. All the three men died of various causes. To face the future, I had to be strong. I was three times widowed. What a challenge in life for a young woman to be facing? I got married to my first husband at twenty-two years of age. A year later I had a baby girl. The following year my husband was involved in a car accident and died on the spot. Heartbroken and challenged, I had to struggle to pick up the pieces and move on. I went for another two years as a single mother and then I met someone I loved.

The urge to get married again set in. I hated being single. I got married again at the age of twenty-six. My husband was a handsome man who worked as a teacher at a nearby primary school. I counted myself lucky because teaching was a respected profession. I thought I had won the jackpot. All was going well until he started to drink a lot. I noticed a lot of things changing in my life and around me. Sometimes he came home late after work or he never came back. Asking where he had been often landed me is serious trouble. We had many arguments and this became a constant occurrence. Each time I asked why he wasn't coming home, he would get very angry. I didn't know the worst was to come.

When he was late home, I knew he would always be drunk and totally wasted. The man I loved turned into an abusive, arrogant alcoholic. He became a rapist and a wife beater. In a week I could be raped several times. If I tried to refuse, I would be beaten up to the extent that I could not go to work. The physical bruises and swelling on my face did not bother him. Why would it? Sometimes he would beat me up and I would bleed and pass out on many occasions.

Many problems arose after. We both started missing work. He was always drunk so he couldn't go to work and because I had been beaten up badly, I could not face my work colleagues. This carried on for over a year. The school authorities where he worked noticed that he turned up for work drunk. He was given several warnings but he didn't heed them. He was eventually fired. He dumped all his frustrations on me. The alcoholism continued and got worse. He was now drinking daily. He beat and raped me daily, accusing me of sleeping with everyone at work. It got so serious to the point of threatening me with a knife. That's when I decided, 'Enough is enough'. I had to tell someone in case the worst happened. On one occasion I slept outside the house. He could not remember the reason I didn't sleep in our home.

My daughter was in boarding school and doing very well. But I rarely saw her during the holidays as she preferred to spend time with my father or my brothers. She could not see much of what was going on and what I was going through. In any case, I didn't want to expose her to the abuse that I was facing. I was also afraid that she would get abused like I was.

I shared my plight with my friend and neighbour. She could not believe that my husband, who appeared to be a quiet man to everyone, could do that. She told the story to her husband who was a police officer. They called me into their house one afternoon and the husband took a statement from me. He assured me that he would come to rescue me if I ever get beaten up again. It wasn't a matter of if I get beaten up again, but when. The police officer gave me a small key ring which I had to press the next time my husband beat me up.

The key ring would trigger an alarm in their house. We didn't have to wait long. Before the end of that week my 'normal' routine of rape started. When I resisted the rape by pushing him away, he started beating me up. I remembered to press the key ring. The police officer next door came in and arrested my husband. The case was brought before the court and he was found guilty and sentenced to six months in prison.

I took his absence as an opportunity to get rid of him. I packed all his clothes and belongings and took them to his family. After serving his time, he was barred by the police from setting foot anywhere I lived or worked. I was happy to be a free woman again at the age of twenty-eight. This is how my second marriage collapsed, just like that.

I stayed single for another three years before loneliness kicked in again. This time I was rather desperate, thinking I was getting too old. I was feeling the pressure from family and church members and felt that society was judging me harshly.

At the age of thirty-three I met another man, a divorcee with three children. I quickly jumped into marriage again because of pressure from society and because I felt I was getting old. The first two years of marriage were great. But things started to change in the third year. This man had a transport business. His trucks transported crops and grain from farms to the Grain Marketing Board in the capital city for processing. Like my previous husband, he started spending nights away from home on the pretext that he was working. When I asked why he wasn't spending nights at home, he would get annoyed and go away for a week or two. When he finally came home, he would infect me with all sorts of Sexually Transmitted Infections (STIs). I had endless trips to hospital for treatments. I had discomfort in my tummy, discharge from my private parts, and painful genital swelling. I knew this was not right and had to do something about it. The doctors gave me several warnings.

I later discovered that my husband was sleeping with several women, but it was rather too late. The women started harassing me and they would call the house phone looking for my husband. We had many arguments because of the women calling, but also because I was refusing to sleep with him. I had been warned by the doctors of the high risk of getting infected and getting ill from STIs again. I was also being beaten up and on occasion he would out after beating me up, to sleep at one of the girlfriends' house. I 'accepted' this behaviour as normal, again. I was fed up! But I could not see a way out and I was worried at how family and friends would view me if I got divorced again.

Things got really bad when one day I came back from work and noticed that he and the kids were gone. That was husband number three gone. I was alone again and afraid to face the world. Two months later I heard that he had been admitted to an infectious diseases hospital. I went to see him, not because I loved or cared for him. I went to tell him that I was pregnant. When I saw him, he was nothing but skin and bones. He had become very skinny and dark. I could not recognize him. I took one glance at him and threw up. I could not even mention the purpose of my visit. I was shocked! And I was distraught. My friend held my hand and walked me out. After a while, I went back again to make sure it was really him not a ghost. I was even more confused and horrified.

I left the room where he was and went to ask the doctors what was wrong with him. The doctor nonchalantly replied,

"AIDS!" "What?" I could not believe my ears. I was shocked and immediately felt sick. I was confused and could not make sense of anything. My mind was all over the place. I felt like a zombie and started to hallucinate in broad daylight.

After several days of pain and agony, my friend booked me an appointment to go and see a doctor. The appointment was for the following week. I lost the pregnancy due to stress. At the same time, I found that I was HIV positive. To add salt to the wound, I also discovered that my husband had passed away in hospital. It was very overwhelming to deal with the speed at which events were going.

I kept asking to myself, 'Now who can tell me how to handle this?'

'How on earth can I tell someone my story?' I pondered. 'Who would want to be near me if they knew what I have been through?'

During that time the HIV/AIDS pandemic was rife. The stigma was unbearable. People were dying in large numbers. At the cemetery, funeral processions were given time slots, and there were queues of families waiting to bury their loved ones. I found myself lonely and suicidal. I wanted to kill myself to escape the shame and the pain. I was angry and frustrated. I could not understand what I had done wrong, why my life should be cut short because of love. There was no support system available. It was impossible to discuss my condition with my family. I was shaking daily. I completely lost my mind. And I was now dealing with my crisis secretly and that made the pain even worse. All I was thinking about constantly was, 'I'm about to die' or 'I am paranoid' or 'I'm stuffing food, so I am maintaining good weight'. The mirror became my best friend and my foe. I kept checking for changes in my figure. I didn't want anyone to say that I was losing weight. I would tell myself, 'At least I'm fat, I am not losing weight.'

They say, 'Trouble comes in threes'. As I was going through all this pain, I received more bad news. My second husband has died due to alcohol poisoning. I now went into a severe depression. The pain was unbearable. If I had been thinking about killing myself, I was now seriously considering suicide as the only possible outlet left to get rid of the pain that I was experiencing. What would anyone do if they were in my situation?

By a stroke of luck I was fortunate meet someone I prefer to call a 'Good Samaritan'. This person took me overseas to Britain where I started to live again. I got access to medication, and became mentally and physically fit and strong. My confidence and self-esteem came back. I started a new chapter in my life, away from the pain and trauma that I had experienced in my country of birth. I felt the urge to help other people who were in my position but not able to get out of their dire situation. I thought my life struggles would inspire them to realise that there is always light at the end of the tunnel. So I started writing books as an escape route from my troubles, but also to help other women who are victims of domestic violence and sexual exploitation. I trained and qualified to lecture in colleges. I am now an author. I also motivate and encourage women to speak up about all forms of abuse. I help women to reinvent their lives and encourage them to seek help when they are in toxic relationships.

I thank God for the opportunity to be able to know Him, get help from church, and hospital with the incredible staff, doctors, nurses, and counselors. I am happy. I have lived for

30 years after my diagnosis. Had I killed myself when I felt suicidal, would I be here helping other women? I am glad I found favour upon my life. I made the right decision to forgive those who put scars in my life. I'm a grandmother. I love life. My mission is not finished until God calls me. Be strong dear reader, dear friend. Do not take your life. Believe in God. He has plans for you and me. My HIV diagnosis was only a scar. For over fifteen years, the HIV virus in my system is not detectable. It's not there. What a wonderful way my life has been. I attribute this to my inner strength to bounce back. Resilience!

TWO

THE CULTURE OF MY LAND

Being single is a curse in my culture at my age. Singleness comes in different forms and shapes. Some people are single by choice. Others are single after a divorce. In addition, some are single after losing their partner. However, in my culture and in my community, you are expected to be single until a certain age.

Most western people would wonder why being single is such a curse. It appears that in my culture, when one reaches a certain age, the norm is to get married and have children. There is nothing wrong with that. After all, most women would love to be married.

I believe God made it clear as He created Adam and Eve. Marriage is a great thing. It has great benefits. However, I seem to be among the growing number of mature singles. I have met rich, poor, educated, illiterate, big, small, ugly and beautiful singles.

All they have in common is singleness. The stigma about mature singleness within my culture seems to be worsening. This defeats the message *'free to be single'*. I would have assumed that this stigmatisation is outdated, especially right now in the 21st century.

It is just so difficult to be in my shoes. It takes courage to begin explaining how I feel about being single at 58 years of age. What happened in my life before, nobody cares or understands. Very few people take time to understand why I am still single at this age. Please people hear me out. I also do not like being single. I wish you could open my mind and read what I am struggling with day in and day out.

I am sure by the time you finish reading this book you will begin to understand why there are so many mature singles. I wish I could go out there and announce some of the challenges about mature singleness to the whole world.

I need to free this from my heart. Sometimes, I wish people could see what is inside my heart and mind. It is not by choice that I am in this situation. This chapter will give you a true picture of how I am feeling inwardly and how it sometimes shows on the outside yet I pretend in order to fit in.

Do you think I do not like companionship?

I often feel that society looks at me differently. Wherever I go, I seem to see shadows of people drifting away from me. I have often wondered if it would have been the same if I were married like 'them'. Then I ask myself, 'Do they know my story?' No, they do not!

I have asked myself repeatedly why I cannot come out with the right answer to this million-dollar question: 'Why is being single made a curse?'

I know some of you are my friends. You have been fortunate to be married. I have done that before and had a nasty experience. I am so aware that we are all fearfully and wonderfully made, bearing in mind, 'Beauty is in the eye of the beholder!'

So why do my friends make it so difficult for me to live? I have made up my mind to speak out today! My story will make you understand why I am single.

I want the world to start seeing mature single people with some sort of respect and dignity and stop calling us names. I am not saying all single people experience this stigma and persecution, only a few feel the same as I do. This is my story, my journey and my experience. This is my story based on the pressures in my culture.

Please stop seeing me as an outcast. I did not choose to be single. I want to be like you my friends! Remember I was married three times and my experience was unbelievable.

Being from Africa, the cultural expectations are for me to do the right thing at some point in life. As a young girl going through puberty in high school, a lot of aunts and uncles were already giving me counsel on ideas of what was expected of me in life. This counsel included how I should prepare to be a good wife, how to prepare for sex life as a married woman, how to respect the in-laws and what was expected of me as a married woman in the community. Boys were counselled on how to be responsible husbands and to be the lead person with more say in the family.

At this stage, we were all at par. That is the norm and I salute it because it teaches the morals of our culture. If one comes from a poor background the whole family would be looking forward for the day their girl child would get married. Marriage was a form of surety for a better life for that particular family. The patriarchy would benefit through giving away the poor child in marriage. This changed the financial situation of that family because of the dowry they charged. We call it *lobola*. It is some form of bride price traditionally paid with cattle by the groom to the bride's parents. This is still practiced today but money is now used. This is quite an interesting and elaborate ritual that involves the aunts and uncles from the bride's side gathering around to discuss how much the husband to be has to pay as bridal price.

Some families charge a bride price so exorbitant that their daughter effectively becomes a slave to the family she marries. Because of this, they would have in a way, sold their daughter and is enslaved by the new husband's family. In some families, the experience was so challenging and daunting that the new bride was expected to work in the field as a way of recouping what the in-laws charged.

Some families charged up to five or ten herd of cows. Amongst all the things, the aunts and uncles will be celebrating the good job they had done to raise a beautiful girl with good morals and good behaviour, someone who has not shamed them. They will make their demands on the day when *lobola* is paid. In my culture, I am not only my parents' child when it comes to the day of charging *lobola*. I belong to the whole village, to my community and the village has a right to demand what they feel is reasonable from my husband on that day.

Not all communities or tribes in Zimbabwe follow this practice. Some tribes have more methods that are modern and are not so primitive. Things have changed. However, although there have been these shifts, there are people who still cling on to them in order to marry their child. There may be pressure from more senior members of the family to comply with family or community values. In case I fall ill or die, God forbid, without such rituals having taken place there will be problems, the uncles and aunts would boycott my funeral.

Such a boycott is aimed at punishing my parents for acting on their own and not consulting them. The parents get this sanction from the village and oftentimes have to deal with such trauma by themselves. This sanction is also aimed at sending a signal to other families in the community that they should not do this in the future.

On the day of marriage, the uncles and aunts would bring out a big shopping list demanding groceries, beers and wines so they get drunk and be merry. Some relatives, who have never had the chance to drink quality beer, will do so on that day. There will be dancing and stripping because of intoxication with many people drinking beers that could never afford in their life. On that day my parents have very little to say, except that they are given the opportunity to say what they want their son-in-law to give them before the gathering. Most in-laws demand their own cows, in addition to what the uncles and aunts demanded.

To my surprise, the in-laws are given authority to lead the whole ceremony and charge the son-in-law. The cows demanded would not necessarily go to them, but they can have them on lease. If they need to plough their fields, they can go to their son-in-law's house, take the cows for work, and then herd them back after the ploughing.

However, in some instances, the in-laws may want to slaughter one of those cows for meat or may want to retain them for the future. In this case, the father of the bride would notify his family of his intentions. Normally he would be given two to four cows for himself, so he could use them to feed his family and in ploughing the fields. The mother of the bride is allowed one female cow that has not given birth yet. This symbolism of this cow is that the bride is still a virgin and she will bear children for the husband. In addition to providing these cows to the bride's family, big jackets and thick blankets of considerable value would also be demanded by the girl's parents. These are of symbolic value – to protect the parents of the bride in the winter.

On the day of the *lobola* payment, the husband –to-be has to come prepared with a reasonable amount of money that they should pay on the day. The tradition is that the aunts give a hint to the representatives of the groom as to roughly how much he will be expected to have to cover the charges on the day. The money varies according to families. The greatest determinant of the amount depends on how the parents want to benefit from their daughter's marriage. Poor families want to change their status so they tend to charge enough t make a change in their lives. After that, the sisters of the girl who is being married also get to say how much they get to 'pick' from the amount which their sister has shown to them. The money came from her husband-to-be. The bride was expected to show to her aunt the money that would be offered to the sisters beforehand.

The reason for this practice was to help the bride's siblings. It was also payment for their time as they played a role in the marriage. Sibling sisters help their sister when she goes to live with her husband and the new family. The sisters accompany the bride until she settles in the new family, so by right they also get a share of the money used for *lobola*.

On the husband's side on the day of *lobola*, he is expected to bring his family members to help with the formalities. They act as negotiators during the negotiations of *lobola* amounts. The husband-to-be is not allowed at this first meeting so he has to send his representatives. Therefore, he sits in a different room. His uncles are the only people who are allowed to meet the bride's family at this first face-to-face meeting where negotiation of prices takes place.

This whole exercise, think of it, commodifies the girl. The bride is treated like a piece of meat. To have people sitting down and negotiating how much a girls is worth and how much they should pay for her to go and be with the other family, is the ultimate insult to the girl.

Once they have agreed the price, the bride's father is asked if he is happy and satisfied with what the uncles have decided to charge for the girl. In some families, the tradition is different. Not everything is negotiated on the day of the *lobola*. In this instance, they arrange with the bride's father beforehand and have an idea of how much he wanted to be paid. On the day of the *lobola* payment, the father of the bride does not speak much and only agrees if he is happy with what is charged by his representatives.

The mother of the bride has little say in the *lobola* negotiations. She is expected to agree with whatever is given to her. She can only demand clothes and her sisters demand cows, blankets and jackets for her. It is a very interesting occasion. Once all the *lobola* has been listed down and the reasonable amount of money paid, the son-in-law is now called in from the other room where he was all this time away from the proceedings. The newly married girl is asked to go and give drinking water to the husband to be. Drinking of this water symbolises an agreement to enter into marriage.

This is the time the aunts and uncles and everyone else to enjoy themselves after all the formalities. Music is played at full blast to announce to people that their daughter is now married to a new family. Introductions are carried out, gifts exchanged, and members of both families are brought together to form one large family. Introductions include everyone from the youngest child, uncles, aunts and even neighbours are included. This is done to boast about how big the bride's family is, but also it is a warning to the husband that if he fails to look after his wife, the 'daughter of the village' they are many eyes that will be looking and many people that will come for him. The husband's family understands the symbolic value of a large family.

The parents of both the husband and wife are also formally introduced and they have a chance to greet each other and hug one another. The party continues with beer drinking and a lot of food served. Usually a goat is slaughtered for meat and the two families have a meal together as a sign of coming together in unity.

It is after the party that the girl's family will remind the new husband's family to try to bring the rest of the *lobola*, and the cows in a few weeks or months to come. The husband is also reminded that he should take good care of the wife since she will be leaving her family to join her new one. Most people will not pay all the *lobola* within the time given. This is a deliberate practice. The husband's family wants to find out if the wife can bear children for them. In case she does not, there would be pressure from the husband's family to find another woman for him. If the woman has children for him, the rest of the lobola is paid without any issues.

In order to have a white wedding after payment of lobola, the husband will formally seek approval from the wife's family. They can only do this if all the lobola has been paid. Only a few people pay up lobola and demand a wedding. White weddings are culturally not that important. The most important issue is to ensure that lobola demands are met. A wedding too is a bonus.

Some days after the payment of *lobola*, the aunts of the married girl accompany her to the new home where she will live with her husband. There are rituals that have to be followed on arrival at the family home for the first time. The bride is covered with a white sheet, a symbol to the man's side that they have brought them a virgin. The family of the husband does not just unveil the sheet to see their new daughter-in-law. They have to dance and sing for the new bride; paying some money to the aunt to remove the sheet from her face for everyone to see her.

The girl's aunt is the one in charge after the unveiling of the bride. She checks to see that the money is reasonably fair, and then she removes the veil or cover from the girl's face. This is the permission to show off the new bride to the in-laws child. A second celebration then takes place which involves introductions and song-and-dance to welcome the daughter in-law to her new family. As this is the first time at the in-laws' house as a married woman, the bride can now sleep with her husband. Remember *lobola* was charged on the assumption and assurance to the in-laws that their son was marrying a virgin. The proof of the pudding now has to be revealed.

If by any chance the bride was not a virgin and her new husband chose to embarrass her, he could now tell the girl's aunts that she was not a virgin. On some occasions, the husband may not want to reveal the secret of the wife's virginity, but the aunt puts him on the corner to reveal it anyway. With the tables turned, the husband's family could go back to the girl's family and notify them that their girl was not a virgin. This is not done verbally but through ritual. They take back to them a new white bed sheet. Choosing white is symbolic. It is meant to send a signal to the parents of the girl that their child was not a virgin. A big hole is cut in the centre to show and shame the girl's family that their daughter has already slept with other men before the marriage. This brings a shame to the family. At this point, the parents' hope is that their child will be able to bear them children.

After that first night, the following morning the daughter-in-law is expected to perform certain chores. The girl's siblings, who would have accompanied her to the in-laws' house, are expected to help their sister. The chores they perform include going to the well early in the morning to fetch water for every member of that family to bath; and grinding millet from a rock using a small stone to turn it into mealie-meal. As a daughter in-law, you are expected to go and fetch firewood in the bush and come home to make a fire and warm that water for the family to bathe. The daughter-in-law is also expected do all the cooking and washing of the dishes.

The in-laws do not just bath and say, 'Thank you!' They have to put money in a bowl after bathing and after eating. This is a way of appreciating and accepting of the new daughter-in-law into their family. This is very important as the bride feels she is accepted into her new husband's family. From this point onwards, all the chores are left for the bride to perform. This is a test to see whether the daughter-in-law had a good upbringing and was taught how to be a proper and well-cultured wife.

THREE

MAKE HAIL WHILE THE SUN IS SHINING

After all that had happened to me in the past, I thought my life had ended. I was hopeless, yet God had a plan for me. I did not know there could be life after troubles; and life that is so sweet and so worthwhile to live again. I thank God for being saved. However, I had to open my eyes and fight all my troubles. I needed to be a woman of virtue to overcome the pain and suffering that I was going through. Miracles do indeed happen. I know God does things in a way that no one can understand. What I know is that the devil comes to steal, kill and destroy. So who am I to skip that if my life was so twisted? I now have every reason to thank God and live a life full of desired Holy spirit, purpose-driven and graceful.

It is when one goes through hell and is toasted in flames of fire, and then manages to come out of it that they realise who exactly they are. Had I still been in and of the world, my life now would have been a living hell. I also thank God for the challenges that gave me the wisdom that I now have.

This book was inspired by a desire to help people out there to understand the nature of the world we live in and why one has to repent to be saved. This world is not fair. I have deceived myself by believing that I am not afraid and I have everything it takes for me to be a great woman. After all my struggles, I have been trying to please my family by following the norm, following what society expected of me so that I could fit in. I have been trying to live my life following family values, as expected by society.

I can handle peer pressure with no problem and can somehow manage it. However, shaming my parents has never been one of those choices. I was always under pressure to get married as expected from a good and exemplary child. Hence, I was getting married very quickly, jumping from one failed marriage to another. The only marriage I really cherished was the first one. My first husband left me to pick up the pieces with my daughter after he was tragically involved in a car accident with an army vehicle. That was the only person I really loved, and he is gone and never to be seen. I mean he is dead and buried, literally.

The ensuing years were a struggle. Getting to understand that he was gone for good was very difficult to take and understand. He was the man who broke my womanhood, so he always had, and always have, a special place in my heart. He is the one whom I loved, the father of my child and my childhood sweetheart. However, he left just like that. How can one move on at twenty–two years of age, widowed and with a child? My heart burst with open wounds and still bleeds from the inside.

They said it never rains; it pours heavily. Everything happened as I was beginning to enjoy my marriage. Then all of a sudden my life changed ad had to find alternative accommodation. It all looked awkward for me going back home and live with my parents again. I become a child again to my parents. It was painful to leave all the things I had worked for with my husband to his family and go back home with nothing except my clothes and my child to start afresh. All my friends from previous years when I was still at my parents had moved on and had no-one to lean on. They had either been married or had just matured and moved on with their lives. I had to look around to find new friends and at the same time get used to living with mum and dad at their house again.

Even if I wanted to live by myself then it was impossible to think of it. This was an odd case of a child taking care of another child. I did not have much to offer the child I had brought to the world, except love. It was great to get some help from my parents, as the job I had did not pay enough to give me an independent life to be a single parent. Thank God, for my parents who accommodated me and were feeding me once again. In those two years, I worked and struggled to make ends meet.

I worked extremely hard for a housing allocation department of the City Council. Then the unexpected happened. I was extremely fortunate to be allocated a flat in the city centre and really pleased. I just had a life passport to freedom again. As I brought the news to my parents, they were happy and excited for me that I had moved on. However, there was still some lingering pain. I did not have over the death of my husband and no one knew how I was bleeding inside my heart from this loss. I was faking happiness all the way. This was the courage of the weak. I became deceitful trying to hide my pain, constantly being in denial of the truth. If only I had let my feelings out or spoke to a professional about my pain, maybe it would have helped soothe the pain, and eased my heavy heart which was constantly bleeding.

Time passed and the pain did not recede. Days, weeks, months and years went by. I still was not telling myself the truth that would help my situation. As loneliness kicked in again and still looking beautiful and healthy, I now thought of finding someone to love me. Loneliness was tearing me apart. It was shocking how quickly the men came when I put myself out there as young as I was. I was beautiful, but I was also choosy. That was the power I only exercised – the power of choice. I found power knowing that getting what I wanted out of my beauty was never a hard thing to do. Men were still fighting to see who could win me. I was like a lucky ticket to Heaven for them or a honeybee to be precise. I also took advantage and used my beauty as a ticket to love. Whatever I wanted, it was a question of whom to pick and out of them and ask them to deliver. As for them, too they knew if they do not deliver, they would be kicked to the kerb.

How happy was I then if you ask me? I was very happy with the power of choice in my hands. Authority and power makes life easy. However, when people know that you are searching for the wrong thing, they will also use you and abuse you. They play on your vulnerabilities. For years, I enjoyed getting all the things I wanted through love, power and authority. However, that was deceitful. I never dreamt of long term goals in life. Everything was about instant gratification.

One lesson that I learnt was that all that glitters or is attractive would fade and get rusty one day. I was the Queen of Sheba then and could get away with murder. I exchanged my beauty for vanity. I thought that would last forever. When things are like that, do you know who brings the most expensive gifts to you? Wealthy married men. They do not care because they lose nothing by using you and abusing you too.

I would love to urge all the young girls to take care of themselves. Life will not remain the same. We grow old and weary. The body loses its shape and goes south. Not everything will remain aligned and when you get shapeless, you will see the true picture of love. Listen to the wise woman. All the looks will fade and the nice structure that you have now will disappear into thin air in ten to twenty years time. All the games you play now will be no more. No one will even dream of taking you out for tea, let alone do things for you. If you can, find your own man now and settle for the right reasons. Make hay while the sun shines, before it gets darker. However, do not deceive yourself. Find love and settle only with the right intentions. Let God guide you in making decisions and choices. I love you and I will forever say things that will help you to a better life. I hope you will understand the challenges I faced described in chapters to follow. I hope the experiences will make you wiser in your own journey.

FOUR

HUSBAND NUMBER 2, SHAPIRO 1984

The relationship with Shapiro for me was a match made in Heaven. After years of searching and playing the love game, I knew I had to stop and settle down again. This time I was only twenty-six years old. "Shapiro, oh Shapiro," I would say to myself in reference to a man who was a teacher by profession. He was very handsome and stood at six feet tall. What a jackpot I had won. I never looked back when I fell for him. Any woman would have fallen in love with Shapiro because of his handsomeness. He knew how to handle a woman. Whenever I saw him, I would melt. I worshipped him like a living god. He swept me off my feet at first sight. I still remember vividly how a great kisser he was. If I was asked to rate him, I would put him at a whopping 150 percent.

Shapiro was well spoken and knew how to handle even women who thought they were high class. I thought I was. I carried myself with some sophistication that was also deceitful. I used my beauty to try to negotiate my life's future without any wisdom. Shapiro would play the game with more experience than I would. He knew all the nicest places in the city where he could go to sweep a girl right off her feet. I was also easily persuaded because of lack of wisdom.

Although I was only a secretary at work, I knew how to take care of myself and fit in with whoever would come from the highest level of class and be one of them. When I dressed up and looked in the mirror, I would also see myself as a living angel. I may be speaking to someone in that position right now. My warning to them is that be very careful, as this game will soon finish before you even realise. You must be humble and not deceive yourself and believe that you are high and mighty. We tend to focus on wrong things when we are that young and tender age. Never forget where you come from and do not let the world run your life. Do not race the world. Let the world race you. I thought I was right. I was not. I was wrong. Now I know.

It takes a little moment just to focus on what your parents preach to you day in and day out. I understand that when you are at that age you would try to conform to your peers. Let us not forget those peers have different experiences and come from different backgrounds. We live in a world today where most of the homes are broken. Some are single parent families due to death like my experience. Some never chose to get married but had kids anyway. They bring them up single-handedly. Some got married and divorced, are separated and some became single parent families through the death of one the parents. Circumstances, therefore, are bound to be different.

Where is Christ in all this? He is there. He is watching but you only need to seek Him and find Him.

We had good times with Shapiro. My luck was that of every single girl. This was my wish. Shapiro was a man of every woman's dream, I should say. He was handsome, tall and loving. However, this was all a smokescreen. I had my own blinkers, paralysed by naivety, youth and love. It only took two years before I started seeing the deceitful reality. As Shapiro was working a few miles out of the city, he could use public transport to go to work and back. We had no car. I was working in the city – just a walking distance from my city council flat.

One day, Shapiro asked for my hand in marriage. It does not matter how old one is, you still have to follow tradition and get married. The ritual of paying money, cows and all those nice things to the bride's family were completed. I was now married. However, Shapiro had no home of his own so he moved to live with me in the flat. There was trouble ahead.

Zimbabwean culture states that when a woman gets married, she has to move to the husband's home. This practice has changed and the opposite now happens as well. I am not speaking of the modern life but that of the 1960s when I was born. The man can now move in with the woman in her house. This makes it easy for me to see that what glitters is not gold. Although he was a teacher, it was just a profession. He was in serious financial problems and nearing bankruptcy. That brought many problems at the age of twenty-six, a child and a husband. We both could not support the lifestyle he had shown me during the time of courting. There was now tension in the marriage and emotional and psychological abuse started rear its ugly head.

The love never felt the same when we started living together. To make matters worse, I always compared him with my late husband. They were never meant to be the same, but his cruel actions did not help. I guess I got into this tangle, as it felt like I was running out of time. I kept on thinking that I would not find anyone willing to marry me as a single parent, but that was just 'culture pressure'. Therefore, by marrying this man, I thought I would solve my problem of being single and relieve the social pressure that I was facing. I also thought that I would avert the loneliness problem I was facing. I thought that I had found happiness. Poor me! That was not the case. He was also an alcoholic. Being handsome was his ticket to promiscuity. He was a womaniser!

Getting married to him meant I had to go through *lobola* again and doing the chores and proving again to this new family that I was a great woman who respected cultural values. The families might be different but the expectations are similar even though I got married in a different part of the country. The irony was that I was young and needed a husband, but he was never there all the time. He was always at the pub drinking with his friends and girlfriends. I joined him in drinking so we could be together all the time. I lost most of myself for the time I was married to him. I cannot recall how many times we fought. We never had a good marriage. I wish I knew what I know now.

Maybe it would have been a good marriage. I was far away from God. I did not know the best way to conduct myself especially when confronted by him. At the end of 1987, I had chosen to keep quiet if there was any abuse. I was afraid of losing him and being by myself again. That was beginning of a new round of abuse, albeit from another husband. Those days church was considered only for poor people or those people without family. We missed the place where we could get help and relied on the world. How good was the world to me? We had lived life in the fast track with little knowledge of the future. I wished there was a school called, 'How to make your life and marriage work'. However, there was not. I relied on my poor aunts who were also very poor. They could only see their having a better life once she was married. It seemed there was no way out for a woman.

Everyone believed that I had a better chance in life as I was married to a teacher. Everyone thought I had a better life prospects than any of my peers. In Africa, there is a saying in vernacular which translates to "What covers the roof of your house is Heavens". The meaning of this is that whatever goes on in your household is a secret and no matter how you struggle, you should keep it quiet. That is what a strong woman does. This was not for me. I struggled. I was not strong.

It now became so bad that Shapiro started to drink so much that we had arguments nearly every night. The drinking became routine. He would get home after midnight every day of the week. Once he was drunk, no one in the house slept. I used to go to sleep early, trying to be ready for work the following morning but he would not allow that.

When he came home at midnight, he would start singing at a very high voice so that I would not sleep. He would play music on full blast and even woke the neighbours up. This went on for a year. As if playing music at midnight was not enough, he would kick me in the back or on the stomach telling me not to pretend to be sleeping.

Using his exact words, he would say "Have you forgotten I paid my money to your family?"

He would add, "Wake up! I want my food. Come on warm it up now. I want to eat."

I was stubborn and sometimes I would rather let him kick me and still stayed in bed. He would strip the blankets off me and use a belt to hit. Many times, I then woke up to warm his food. I did manage to do as I was told in some days, especially when he hit me hard.

This sort of behaviour went on for almost one-and-half years. I felt I could handle it and that it would eventually get better. I kept quiet and hid everything from my family and friends. I did not want my family to see me as a weak woman. Thinking about it now, I thought that was normal for I grew up seeing my parents in a similar abusive relationship. In my mind that was somewhat normal.

It became worse, to the extent that when he came home before even saying anything to me I would jump and start doing everything for peace's sake. Once he had eaten, he would sleep on the sofa forgetting I was in the house too. Sometimes I could just let him sleep there so I could have my peace. However, when he woke up he would start drinking again if there was any beer in the fridge. That became normal for me. When he wanted to sleep with me, it was not love anymore but rape. We only had sex when he felt like it. I had no choice in the matter.

I then started to get fed up with it and started refusing and pushing him away. I remember one day he bit me when I refused him sex. I was bleeding from nose and the whole body was sick. I could not go to work the following morning. I had to lie that I was sick so I could heal.

I became a slave in my own house. Thank God, I had sent my daughter to boarding school so she was not seeing the abuse-taking place. During holiday time, she would go to my dad's house or my brother's. That way my family would not really know what was happening to me.
It became so serious that he also had started missing his work because of drinking. The school began to notice that he was coming to work drunk sometimes. He was then suspended for a month. They asked him to sort his life out and become organized. He never did. He was now alcoholic, abusive, violent and a rapist.

My life became a living hell. If I survived a day, it would be a great day for me. Going home for me after work did not give me a good feeling. I would be expecting a hiding or having no sleep at all. This was routine for me. I began to lose interest in and with everything. I was not surprised when I started wetting the bed at night from anxiety. I was scared and had nowhere to run to.

By the end of 1987, I had had enough. This time around, the abuse was becoming very serious. If I did not open the door in time, he would jump on my throat trying to squeeze me to death. I would have to wrestle with him and since he was drunk, he could fall easily. Oftentimes, he would then fall asleep there on the floor.

I knew something serious would happen to me and none of my family would know. One day he came back from another round of drinking. Without even knocking on the door for me to open for him, he instead broke the window and tried to get in through that window. When I stopped him from doing that, he took a sharp knife from the kitchen and wanted to attack me with it. When I noticed this, I ran out of the house. I saw a different Shapiro on that day.

That incident was the final straw for me. I could not help it but run to the caretaker's flat next door who helped me together with his wife by letting me stay for the night in their flat. The next day I went home. He could not remember what had happened.

Such incidents were now becoming routine for me and Shapiro. I would be kicked, raped or chased by a knife being accused of seeing other man and yet I was as innocent as a religious none. The next time he put a knife to my throat. I do not know how I managed to escape from him because he was drunk. As usual, I pushed him and ran away as fast as I could. I could not go to knock next door because I was ashamed and embarrassed. I managed to pull a blanket from the bed and slept outside under the tree.

This episode was another red line for me. I said to myself if I do not seek help, I would die. I told one of my friends who said if it happens, again I should run away and go to her house. Before long, it happened again and I went to my friend's house where she put up with me for the night. She asked me to chase him away from my flat, but after all the abuse I was not sure if that was possible.

My friend told her husband who was a police officer my story. The husband called me one afternoon into their house and took a statement from me. I explained all that was happening to me and what I was going through at home. The couple saved my life. The husband said next time when he starts hitting me I should phone him anytime. I was now feeling a bit better knowing I had someone who knew my predicament and whom I could run to in case of emergency.

After a week of me not sleeping at home, I went back. I knew, however, that he would beat me again once I get home. I did not care anymore. The minute he started beating me and accusing me I called the police officer who came and handcuffed him. That was my saviour and that incident marked the end of my marriage. He was put to prison and never went back to teaching.

That was a second failed marriage for me.

I felt marriage just was not meant for me.

Shapiro the man who had swept me off my feet with love was the man who nearly killed me. My family, up to this time, did not know what was happening or what had happened to me and him. Most of them still thought I cannot keep men because I am rude, obnoxious and do not seem to take anything serious. Maybe now I am rude and defensive, but that is the only way I had to learn to defend myself if I attacked or approached in a way I cannot cope with.

I know I am strong somehow, but having to be beaten up every night or being used as a sex tool in the house was never a good thing for me. I tore me apart. How did I let that continue to happen? Even now, I do not understand it myself. I wonder how I went through all that surely – very quiet and getting beaten up every night, raped and suffocated to near death. The police officer was my only way out of this marriage. Thanks to him, the living Angel.

I would not be here now to write about this if I did not have help from this officer. I give glory to God for strength. Although I still have nightmares, it is very difficult for those nightmares to leave me. It seems to me like I see shadows following me behind, even though this happened some thirty years ago.

FIVE

LOVE AND DECEPTION

What a living hell! After struggles with Shapiro's behaviour and the way he handled our so-called sweet marriage of a match made in heaven, I was tired and vowed I would never get married again. How could I deceive myself I am only twenty-eight when I decided to leave Shapiro? I acted like a tough person, being in my shoes would you forget about love? After all twenty-eight year old women in the western world still focus on their career and have not even started thinking about marriage...

How different is the Zimbabwean society to the western one? I was expected to have raised all my children and looking forward to having grandchildren at my age. Life is very different. I sometimes ask myself why. Is it poverty? Why were we created differently that we run so parallel and yet we live in the same world? I spent most of my early months by myself. I was locked indoors and my heart continued to bleed since I had scarred it.

As I was raised to keep things to myself and not shout to the world about my feelings, I behaved in a manner that my culture requires me to do. Little did I know that I was accumulating a bigger wound in my heart and that one day that wound would fester. Keep reading my story and you will see why I say this. After thirty years of being a single woman, the pressure of being a good African girl nearly killed me.

I tried only to concentrate on my life and that of my child. I was living in the world. I am only human. The problem with my generation is that people find it so easy to label you. As a woman who had been married before, and knows all that it takes for my culture to respect me, the only way to gain some respect was to get married again.

At this age, I am not getting any younger. I am 'very old' according to my culture. Mind you, at fifteen years of age a girl child can be married and have a life with a husband. Let us not forget that as a child in some cases you are forced to marry an older man. Sometimes this man will be older than your own father. You marry them because of family problems or poverty in the family. However, families differ. I was never in that situation, although it was by choice that I conformed to social expectations; or maybe by subtle duress or pressure imposed by society.

The problem I face now is "Why did my parents not stand up for me? Why did they not just say I was not ready?" By accepting these people's money and marrying me, that was consent. I do not hold anything against them anyway. Even if they had wanted to stop me, I do not think they would have succeeded.

The problems of competing with the world is so massive that if one does not stop and think for once they could put themselves into deeper problems. They could end up with scars for life. I have developed scars. Life is hard and unbearable if one chooses the wrong route. As for my fellow young women and young men out there, they should stop and think for themselves. This story is for them to read all the time when they face trials and tribulations in the future. It should be a reminder for them that there is always hope.

SIX

WHAT NEXT SHAPIRO IS GONE?

I was now in my mid-30s and had already married twice. Where were the good men? Was there anything I did wrong? No. I was just unlucky and I was not in good standing with God.

If I had a personal relationship with God, surely things would have been better for me. This was a time when it was easy to find a partner. I was still young and attractive. Men were still getting attracted to me like bees to pollen.

It took me long to recover from my last relationship. I could manage to get a boyfriend here and there. What I did not realise was that time had moved fast. Getting a decent man who could marry me and guarantee a good life was proving to be a challenge. The chances were getting less and less as I got older. It was very scary. Choices were getting limited.

Chances of finding love seemed to be grounding to zero. Time was ticking and it felt so frightening to be alone. My peers, my family and other villagers were beginning to gossip about my situation. They wondered why I was still home. They asked around when I would be getting married. I did not believe I could get married again, but cultural pressure put those thoughts in my head.

I had taken a break from Shapiro and it was now two years later. I could not help feeling insecure. Although I am now relieved in my heart, at that time my heart was pounding with fear. When I look back, I realise that this was natural. I am not made of iron, so these feelings were natural. However, today my heart still is wounded.

I had deceived myself that I would not date again. I desperately wanted someone. Mother Nature dictated my every move. I could not control my feelings. I did not know what to do about sex. Africa is very different from the West where people could go to sex shops and buy sex toys. Shops like Ann Summers is a love toy shop. In Africa, there was none of that at that time. Using sex toys was unthinkable, let alone walking into a shop and buying them. It was considered diabolical. It is perfectly normal for people in the West to buy toys, to have same sex relationships and to remain single. One could be killed for same sex marriages where I come from.

Freedom is very important. I do not blame those people in same sex marriages. I do not know how one ends up in such a relationship, but I cannot judge. Maybe they have been through what I went through and found out that it was better to have a relationship with someone of the same sex. If I had gone through the abuse, violence and rape here in the United Kingdom maybe, I would have considered having a same sex relationship. We all need to be loved and adored.

Taking a break from Shapiro made me very scared. To start again dating again was a nightmare for me. I could not trust anyone. I was suffering from anxiety, panic attacks and insecurity. Everyone I saw was a suspect. I had to be very careful. I was not ready to have sex again. I was afraid.

As I started to open up, my face started to glitter again. I had gone over the pain of the last relationship, but I was beginning to open up. I fell in love with a work mate. We worked together in the same office, but he was in a different department. He had a higher post than me. We dated for a short time and before long, there were lies upon lies. Even though I thought I had had enough of being lied to, I knew something was not right with this one. Experience is the best teacher. His name was Daniel. I can now call him Denial, after all his lies and denials.

We went out together for just over six months. He always came to my flat, but never invited me to his. At first, I thought maybe he does not have a nicer home. I thought he was embarrassed to show me where he lived or maybe that he just loved my place. I was making excuses for him.

He was a married man. He never wore any ring, so I would not have guessed. I just thought my African brothers are like that. That is how they are, not all of them though, but quite a big number has so-called 'spare ribs' outside marriage. I was Denial's spare rib.

It took me some time to know something was going on. I started to work it out upon myself to get the truth out of him. Those days there were no mobile phones, so the idea of phoning him at midnight or texting any time was unthinkable. Mobile phones have made it possible to communicate at anytime. One can text or phone anytime and disrupt the quiet time with the wife. I now know that would have not been the best way to deal with it, but then I had no idea of how to handle a situation with a married man. Those married men who think they are clever would just turn the phone off. In western societies, there is respect for privacy and relationships work on trust. Couples do not usually go through each other's phones so anything could happen. I was different. Because of my insecurity, I would have insisted on going through the phone.

Anyway, I was able to manipulate the situation and get what I wanted from what had now become an affair. We worked together so it was convenient for me. I had nothing to lose anyway. Thinking of it now, I pray that this sort of behaviour should not happen to anyone, to any woman for that matter. Those days HIV and Aids were on the rise. We needed to open our eyes.

My friend who lived next door to him had told me that he was a married man. I had doubts because nearly every Friday he did not go back to his house. We would go out and dance the night away; then he would crash at mine. He made me believe that he loved me.

When I eventually confronted him about his family, he was not very happy. Instead, he went and bought me a very expensive gift to silence me. However, because I had experience from my previous two men, I was now wiser. I knew that was a 'silence present' so I began to plan on how to get rid of him. This was not easy. He was what people call "typical African". When you spend an African man's money, in gifts or any other way during the time you are going out, you will not get rid of them without a fight.

When I told him I wanted to end the relationship, he did not take it lightly. He wanted a fight. I knew at that moment that it was going to be hard to leave him. I had to think ahead. I thought if I made him jealous by telling him that I was over him and was dating someone better than him, he would let me go. That was a big mistake, a terrible one.

One day at a work Christmas party a man who was senior to Daniel at work asked me for a dance. I agreed. That was a mistake. I did not even look at Daniel's reaction because I thought I was over him and he was over me. Again, I was wrong. He stood up from the corner where he was drinking with his friends holding a bottle of beer. He flung it towards me aiming for my face. A work colleague had noticed what he was about to do, so he shouted my name. In panic, I quickly looked back. By a stroke of luck, the bottle missed my face and went on the wall. It broke into pieces.

Why am I telling you all this?

It is because I love you I want you to see the future in you and not focus on the things that will not help your life. I have lived a sad life because of earlier bad decisions and being influenced by the wrong peers. I hope you detect the signs of abuse early in your life and do not have to go through what I went through. In my life, especially during my childhood, I was abused by trusted people. The soldiers who were fighting the Liberation Struggle also abused me. I was a war child.

Daniel was sent to a workers committee. He was reprimanded and told that he would lose his job and stripped of his position if he carried on with the affair. That was the end of the affair.

Can you really blame me? Maybe you could, but I was not aware that he was married. I am human and I was only trying to live a normal life. Not all of us have rosy backgrounds, but we have to make hard choices sometimes and follow a path that is better for our future. As for me, being abused at a young and tender age did not do me any good. I grew up not knowing what love was. I was abused and raped and then made to think that that was love. I lived that sad life, but I have no regrets or hold anyone accountable. I am the one who behaved like that and I would not watch any of the little girls or boys following the route I took and waste their lives.

I have a duty now to educate and speak to the young women. I have to show them better ways of living their lives. I have to counsel and coach them to be better in life. Some choices we make when we are young are deceitful and have consequences throughout our life. I wish I knew all this then. I know my parents tried their best, but I was young and naive to understand what was taking place.

SEVEN

FROM THE FRYING PAN TO FIRE HUSBAND NUMBER 3

The fact that I had suffered domestic violence, abuse and rape did not make me stop dating. I sometimes wonder how we people are created. Even though I had gone through hell and fire with this thing called love, I still did not think it was time to stop.

When I came to this Western world and heard that people could still get married at seventy years of age, I was then able to understand my feelings. I had wished there was a marriage guidance school somewhere. When I saw people marrying at old age, I then understood the turmoil that I was going through. In my culture and society, it was unheard of for people to get marriage at such advanced age.

I think it was my fear of getting old and dying alone. It was fear of loneliness, of not being in love that worried me. I wondered if there was such a thing called love. I thought it was overrated and that people just live together to have children and multiply. I am not under any illusion about the importance of love. It is a very nice thing when it is shared lovingly and when couples care for one another. I can visualise myself in that picture of love. Everyone likes to be loved. Love is sweet, warm, full of passion and care, and is peaceful. I am only sceptical because my experience of love was full of deceit, unkind acts, abuse and cruelty. It was hell.

I could not stay without love. That is the irony of my story. I am not immune to love. I love to be loved, pampered and treated like a queen. I did all this for love. However, I have come a long way chasing love and sometimes I wonder if I will ever get it. My experience of love is being abused, raped and bullied. However, I will not give up. The more they do that to me the more I am determined to be resilient and fight my own way. What do I have to lose anyway?

The only good thing up to today that I thank God for is that I never got pregnant. Despite all these relationships, I never got pregnant. I never brought another life to this earth. I was lucky in that sense. I would have loved to have a big family; but only if had met someone I really loved, but I did not. It was a scary thought to start life with people who cheated and abused me. The good thing about me is that I never give up. I was sure there was someone out there.

I tried so many times to find love, but I could not find it. One of the reasons was that I was not really looking for love. I was chasing approval from my society, my culture. I was trying to please the world; my family and friends. I was deceiving myself, trying to fit in and gain the respect of my culture. All the people I was concerned about and fearful of are not here to nurse my scars today. I took that wrong route, putting strains on my life.

My plea to my dear sisters and brothers, daughters and sons of Zion is that they should rely on God. He is the only one who will show love and give all that they are looking for. There is nothing wrong in staying single and safe. Love is great, but do not force it.

In 1989, I was twenty-nine years old. At that age, I could have given up everything as I had gone through a lot of pain and suffering. I could have surrendered, but i did not. That was the time my body was so ripe that I was desperate to be loved. I began to have those thoughts of finding love or of chasing it. In retrospect, I wish I had never chased it for it came with consequences: scars in my life.

Time went by. I was still working for the City Council in the same housing department. I was very loyal to my job. I spent a good ten years in the same building. I could have spent more than that time in love if I had not lost my beloved first husband, the father to my daughter. It is funny how I could never forget about him all those years. It is true when they say, "The first cut is the deepest".

After my first marriage, my life went on to a halt or a standstill. My first book was entitled *Curse or Blessing Being a Spinster* because I stayed long without love. I had found it at first and then it disappeared. I lost Jonathan and became an unmarried woman. I had never thought that my life would take that route or change in such a dramatic way.

I always had thought of married life with my husband and kids. I never had that. It was just a dream. In my first book, I never detailed my life and what happened because I was afraid of reactions from members of my culture. I was worried about how I would be perceived by society. Even when I had left my own country and come to the West, I still worried about people's perceptions and opinions of me. In this book, I took a new attitude. I said: "To hell with fear. I will conquer the fear now. It is my life, my story. After all it's for educating our dear kids and arise my African women who still suffer or go through what I went through."

This book is for helping others. It is meant to be a revelation. It is meant to show what goes on in life and talk about what people are afraid of talking about. Certain aspects of my culture need to be revisited. They are enslaving. They rule our lives and stop us from making decisions that are right for our lives. Culture is great. It is what binds society, but it should never be enslaving, restricting and imprisoning. I regret not challenging these bad aspects of my culture and going through all this for only to be called a good girl who does not shame his family.

After a few years, I again met Mr Lover-Lover. This time there was no choice. I could not see myself as a person who had a choice considering that time was running out. I was in a rush to get into a relationship, but not because of what I was made to believe by my culture. I was simply thinking that I was twenty-nine years old and time was not on my side. The question that lingered was: "If I don't get married now then what?" In my mind, I strongly believed that there was no way I could get a husband after this age. Remember, I was raised to believe that having a husband was a passport to life. I could punish myself by not eating so I could maintain a great figure so I could get a man.

I was struggling to put food on my table, but I had money for the gym. I needed a great body to make me get a man of my dreams. During those gym times, I met Mr Lover-Lover. I will call him Mr LL. He was not handsome. He was short and scruffy, simply not my type. I just said to me, "Half a loaf is better than nothing." That was because I had spent a long time 'off the shelves,' so to speak. I felt like I was not marketable anymore. I even thought my family would not charge dowry for me; they would simply let me go 'free'.

We dated for a year then the 'M' word, the marriage word, came again. How would I have said no when my mind was telling me that I was off the market? I felt that this was the only way out of the single life that I was living. Mr LL was a divorcee with three children; two boys and one girl. The girl was nine years old. The other boy was seven and the last one was five years old. So overnight, I became a mother of four, including my own daughter who was also seven years old.

I felt complete. As a serial romantic, with hot blood still flowing in my veins, I guess I lied to myself that this was it. I am a woman who needs to be in a sexual and loving relationship. I crave the love and closeness that love brings. I was totally in love with Mr LL and his children. I was under the impression that Number 3 was my lucky number. In Chinese culture, the number 3 is a lucky number.

After being a 'two time loser' it was becoming more difficult to keep blaming the other person entirely, so I took the initiative to make sure that the marriage worked. I had gone from believing that I was invincible to wanting to make it to the 'finish line of life' with some semblance of stability and peace of mind. Then, life is a bitch. It can throw so much at you, leaving you miserable when you had so much optimism.

After the honeymoon period, I was fully ensconced in our new life and new home. My 'Knight in Shining Armour' had introduced me to the joys of sex and all kinds of exciting sexual practices and amazing sex positions. Being a girl growing up in Africa in the 1960s, I was not well versed in this kind of sex.

I thought I had found my soul mate. Then he gradually changed and the green-eyed-monster called jealousy reared its ugly head. He became so controlling and dangerously jealous that whenever he came home from work, the first thing he wanted to do was put his fingers inside me and sniff them. He suspected I was sleeping with other men. I did not understand why and where this was coming from. This not only made me uncomfortable, but also sad that my newly found happiness was going to be short-lived. I could sense that I was on another path to a breakup.

Things started to change. Therefore, at twenty-nine years of age I was a mother of four children. I was effectively playing the role of husband in the household. Mr LL had a small business when I met him. It managed to take care of the family for the first year only. I should point out that he tried his best, but it was difficult. He had his business outside the city so he had to drive long periods to get to work. Managing his business became difficult. Sometimes he could not come back the same day because of lorry breakdowns. The periods of absence became longer. Days turned into weeks. At one point, he did not come home for almost a month. When he eventually managed to come home, he brought no money for the children, for the family. I was the breadwinner and this was beginning to stress me. We were just managing on a very low salary.

This experience was beginning to look like a reflection of my past life. I was worried about his continuous absence from home. My own daughter was at boarding school where I had to pay high school fees for her to stay there. Having an extra mouth to feed and taking responsibility for a whole family was a huge burden on me.

I was tired, won out and fed up of the whole situation. I was losing hope again, I did not know what to do. I constantly worried and had to resolve problems and challenges on my own. I was married, but never saw the husband. The husband never contributed to the upkeep of the family. This felt like imprisonment. I could not go out or do anything. If I had to look after my own child, that would have been bearable, but I also looked after his children.

I am not a selfish person. I could have dumped the kids knowing what was happening in the marriage, but I could not do it. I felt that my obligation as an adult was to protect the children, but somehow I again felt used and dumped. He would come home once a month without money. He did not explain what was happening with him or what was happening with our relationship. I felt unappreciated and taken advantage of.

If I asked what was going on with him, he would get angry. He would leave the house for that day or two and never phone or explain anything. If he decided to leave money, he would calculate what it was for and leave the exact amount and nothing extra. This drained me. I began to get tired again and bouts of panic attacks. Was I wrong or was there something about me which was not right or not normal? I was not sure.

I thought I was being a faithful wife. I was doing everything to take care of his kids and him. I started to face many problems, including health problems. When I slept with him, I would have various problems including tummy aches. I started contracting sexually transmitted infections (STIs) and would find myself visiting the sexual health clinic on many occasions. I could not understand why I was always a victim of such acts. I was being left at home, waiting for diseases to be brought to me.

One thing I know, as I said above, is that when I met him he did not even match my standards. However, I was desperate, so I tolerated him. I groomed him gradually until he started looking sharp. He was now well groomed and was more confident and his self-esteem had skyrocketed. He felt invincible and on top of the world. So now, he had nothing to lose. He had his 'maid' at home, his slave who could run around performing all the chores of a married woman for him.

This did not feel like marriage to me. Well it was not, but we were literally living like a married couple. Now it was beginning to feel more or less like imprisonment. I was house bound because of his kids, although it was in the absence of mine. I was using all my wages to feed his children and put food on the table for him too. What a strange way of showing love. Why did I put up with this?

I was not able to challenge his mean behaviour. I was only happy at work and faced a lot of torment at home. I was full of pretence, making people believe I was happy at home. Everyone thought that I was happily married, yet I was in a mess. Most of my friends thought I was in a great relationship. Again, the pressure brought by culture was there. I could never talk about my situation without being judged.

It is my hope that my sisters, daughters, sons and brothers will not short-change themselves by staying in a relationship that is not working. There are ways of dealing with situations like mine now; for example working with marriage counsellors. If this does not work, they should move on, so that they avoid getting scars like mine. I was lucky to find God. Not everybody does. I get my strength all the time from God. This is my life story. Everyone has their story, but my mission is to inspire other women to be wiser and avoid some of the challenges that affect their lives.

My wish is to create a legacy that abused women can draw from before I leave this planet; whether I am gone or not. I want them to understand that abusive, violent relationships are not to be tolerated at all. We should create more spaces for young people who are abused to confide with somebody and get help. They should not wait to nurse their own death. Each generation should help the other. I was lucky. Had I not found strategies to cope, I would not have been here right now to tell you my story.

I say to young women out there: "Love the person's heart not the looks. Do not be deceived because not all that glitters is gold. Know your enemy. Know the person you are falling for; if it means taking references for love, I would urge you to do so. Stop and think before you marry someone. It is of no use to throw yourself from a frying pan into fire; unless you are prepared to handle the scars. I can assure you that it is painful. You don't want those scars to ruin your life."

EIGHT

EVEN HIS GIRLFRIENDS ABUSED ME

Although I did all the homemaker chores for Mr LL and his kids, it all went without notice. He could not recognise anything I did for him. I was treated with so much disrespect and disdain; with no love, or emotion and no care.

He would be gone for weeks and would call to speak to his kids from wherever he was. I did not mind that, but he would never ask to speak to me. This made me feel cheap and unappreciated. I hated myself. I felt like I had no way out. What made me angry was that whenever he was gone for weeks he would come back and act like nothing happened. I would still cook for him and do his laundry, even though he was showing me lack of appreciation.

The most hurtful thing was I could overhear his girlfriend over the phone screaming to him that he should tell me that it was over. He was no longer interested in me. At first when I heard that, I thought something was wrong with my hearing. What would you do if it were you? I considered suicide, but I was stopped by the thought of my daughter and what fate would be. I worried about the world I would leave for her if I killed myself.

It did not take me long before I snatched the phone from one of his kids and told him to come and pick his kids up. I was not joking anymore. I had had enough of him. I told him I would drop the kids at his mother's house if he did not come to pick them up. He then came back home and apologised as if he had realised his mistakes. I knew it was only for a short while. He was buying time for find a way out that did not disrupt his life and that of his kids.

I realised that there was nothing I was waiting for. There was no love between us anymore and I was wasting my time. There was no longer a marriage. The relationship had died a long time ago. I needed to walk away before it was too late.

The so-called 'long standing girlfriends' were desperate to get married to him. Every time he slept at home, the girlfriends would phone home and ask for him. When I told them that he was not home, there was always a nasty exchange of words. These women would not understand why I was still with him and they would question why I was allowing myself to be used. They would confirm to me the number of days he did not come home and tell me the exact days he did not sleep at home. They would also claim that they were with him in their house.

At first, I did not ask because I was afraid he would go forever. It became worse when the phone calls would come in the wee hours of the morning. He would get up and take the calls in another room. If I asked who he was talking to, he would just walk away and disappear. That routine would take place every time he was home. I ended up not asking. However, even if I did not ask, there was little chance that he would stop his habit. Every time he came back and we had sex, I would end up going to the sexual health clinic.

The fact was that the girls who were calling my house were not lying. If I asked him about the women, he would disappear. I now knew that was his routine. I stopped asking. On one occasion, one of the girlfriends phoned me to tell me what colour clothes and underwear he would be wearing when he came home. This was meant for me to believe this woman.

What do you think happened? Yes, he came home wearing exactly the clothes and underwear that had been described on the phone. This happened on two occasions. What could I do? Who would I tell? It was for me to know the truth. Truth hurts. I now knew where he was and where he performed his so-called work. I was now a full time house cleaner for him and his kids. I felt there was nowhere to run. He had no love for me at all. My heart was scarred and I bled from it.

It now became an intolerable system for me and I became fed up with it. I started refusing to sleep with him. He never bothered anyway because he was having sex somewhere else. He lived a happy double life with no regrets.

I remember one evening coming from work. I parked my car in the garage at the basement of the flat. It was around eight o'clock and not very dark. There were four women waiting for me in the car park. They asked me if I was married and I told them I was. They asked me who I was married to and I mentioned my husband's name. Before I knew it, they started beating me up in that car park and no one was around to rescue me.

I was left bleeding, lying beside my car. They disappeared in a black Volvo. I knew exactly who they were, but there was no need for me to ask my husband because he would deny knowledge of them. After that episode, he did not come home for the next two weeks; so I nursed my wounds alone. Even if I had made an effort to ask, he would not have cared. Therefore, I just kept my mouth shut.

One day I went to work and when I came back, I found the house empty. He was gone. His kids and those few items he had bought for the flat had also been taken. I was pleased in a way, but sad that I had been used. I cried and started picking myself up again as usual. I was now 32 years of age in a culture which stigmatised you if you were widowed and had two divorces under your belt. I was tired. I could not fight anymore. The thought of finding a replacement after this man did not even cross my mind. This time I began to fast and pray feeling sorry for myself. I bled inside.

I honestly believed that I was cursed. Was I? No, I think it was a question of falling for wrong people, without any knowledge of their background and not knowing them well. Most people hide their real selves. Unfortunately, I was going out with people who were leading a double life. I should have taken time to know them well.

As soon as he left, the house felt empty, but I was so pleased to know that the last time I visited a sexual health clinic was when I was with him. I thought everything was fine, but I was to get the shock of my life. It did not last long before I found out that the bugger had left me pregnant. I could not believe it. At first, I thought of having a termination. I was confused. I did not know what to do. I waited and started hunting for him again so I could let him know that I was carrying his baby. I found him at his parents' house one day and told him.

He had the audacity to accuse me of being desperate. He told me directly that he was not interested at all in the pregnancy. When I left his parents' home, I knew that it was my own fault. I had to make a decision. I had no money to go and abort the pregnancy. Even if I had, guilt was killing me and taking an innocent soul was going to be very difficult for me. At least that is how I viewed abortion at that time.

I let it be. One day, four months down the line, I started experiencing some funny tummy aches again; during pregnancy this time. I knew something was so not right. The doctors also said something was not right. They did several tests and told me it was not good news at all I needed treatment.

I suffered for some months then felt like I had healed. Two months later, I went back to work. A friend of mine said I had lost a lot of weight. I carried on doing my work as usual. After six months, my friend went to visit her cousin at the hospital which was an infectious diseases hospital. Coincidentally, she met Mr Lover-Lover. He was lying on a hospital bed. He was admitted in the same ward with her cousin whom she was visiting at that time.

As she came back from lunch, she was very concerned, judging from the look on her face as she approached my desk. She asked me to come with her to her office. She told me she had met Mr Lover-Lover at the hospital on admission and he was not looking good at all.

She said she would not advise me to go and see him as he looked poorly and very different. He had lost a lot of weight and had gone very dark in colour, and was skinny and bony. I told her she should take me to hospital so that I could see him. That evening we went together to the hospital.

When I arrived, I thought we had missed him and that he must have been discharged. The bed that he was supposed to be lying in looked empty. My friend told me he was there, pointing at a heap of blankets. I could not believe it. I thought she was crazy. As we got nearer to the bed, she pulled the blankets. I was shocked to see him there.

All I can say is. This was not Mr LL. This was just a heap of bones. I remember shaking and could not believe my eyes. I trembled for some minutes. I threw up right there not because I had eaten anything bad, but I had seen what looked like a ghost. I asked him why and what had happened. He could not give me a proper answer. He was shy and tears rolled on his face.

I just said to him I had no energy to fight him back. Only God was going to fight my way. I told him that I had lost the baby. He did not seem to care or maybe he did not hear me for he was not even looking at me. I am sure he must have lost his memory or maybe he was now beginning to have some remorse. I was speaking to a 'living corpse'. However, no matter how sorry I felt for him, I needed to think of myself and not him.

Giving him a second glance made me throw up again. Nurses rushed with a bucket this time to me, not to their patient. I said to him, "May you ask God to forgive you? I will never come back here to see you again." I told my friend that we should leave. On my way back to the office, I lost myself a bit. My thoughts reeled back to the hospital and back. I was lost again in different places, broken to pieces. Fear gripped me and I felt angry at the thought of dying in a similar way. My daughter, my family, how was I going to reveal such horrific news to them? Stigmatised! I would be the talk of the town. What was I going to tell people about what I was going through?

I was hurt and afraid. The thought of me dying in a similar way just could not leave me. I was not able to eat or do anything. The thought of suicide occupied me. I became extremely depressed and wanted to take my own life.

All that I was thinking of now was how I was going to die. I did not want to be that skinny and have people visit me in hospital dying. I was worried about my daughter, thinking who would raise her when I die. I could not discuss or tell any of my family members what I had seen at the hospital: a moving corpse. I feared that I would be stigmatised. A month later, news came to me that he had died. One of his kids, the big girl, was now thirteen years old. She came to tell me the news. I told her I was sorry but that I would not be attending her father's funeral. I was hurting and feeling guilty at the same time. I was confused.

Surely, they could not blame me. He was the one bringing all sorts of diseases to the house and his girlfriend was calling my house. I was in fact his house cleaner not his wife. He had brought this illness in my life and why was I going to bury him. I was not to blame and I wondered why I was feeling guilty.

I was actually expecting his parents to come and explain to me or even to inform me of what had happened, but nothing happened. No one came to me. They buried their son. That was the official way to do it. He had been so ill that it was said the body would decompose within a day, so they buried him quick.

After this incident I wondered, "Right what do I do?" I was now widowed for the second time. Although I was not with him anymore, I was still a widow for the second time. "What is my title now? I had been widowed twice and had one divorce. If it was you my friend having this challenge, what would you do?"

I went into a serious depression. Depression does not stop without counselling, I was to find out decades later. Instead, it becomes worse. I thought more and more about suicide. It was now almost inevitable that I was going to take my own life. I think I now had a psychological problem. I consistently weighed myself and for sure, I was losing weight and was not sure of what I should do now.

I started eating for comfort so that I could not loose myself and lose weight at the same time. I did not want anyone to say I was losing weight again. I was secretly staffing food and made sure I pile on some weight.

The year went by without much drama. My battle with my mind continued. I was taking baby steps to getting back to some semblance of normality. My weighting was picking up. The suicidal thoughts were fading. I also started to find myself again. I was now living again. However, any little illness I feel today, I just head straight to the doctors I am in doubt of myself.

Why life has to be so unfair? Why does it always rain on me? What have I really done wrong to deserve this? Where would I go from here? Who would I tell what was happening with me? What will they think about me? If you were me, what would you do?

"I have nowhere to run! It is my fault. I will have to deal with it myself." This was the continuous thinking of one individual who could not discuss anything with anyone. The musing continued: "I am now by myself once more and coming to terms with my life scars. My story is difficult to share, so I am harbouring a secret for life. Do you know how painful it is to keep a secret of a something so terrible? I am afraid to talk to anyone and let them know what I am going through."
The personal conversation continued: "Life has become so hard, especially when I have to fake it so much. I am very

lonely and cold inside. Although my heart bleeds daily, I have to pretend it is alright. Surely, this is the time I wish my family could listen to me. My being a responsible girl has landed me in a painful and tortuous life. Only God knows what I am going through."

While I was going through this personal turmoil, something happened. I met someone else. Before I had met this man, I made a promise to myself that I would never date a liar. I was still young to be short-changed by a lying and cheating man. I finally got involved with a man, who appeared to be a saint. He was working at a diplomatic mission in Africa. Life seemed sweet. My luck had shifted for the better this time. We had great moments with this man and I felt like I had myself a good catch.

He introduced me to a life of luxury, high-class life. I quickly got used to the pampering and the attention. However, unbeknown to me, a man who had swept me off my feet and who had introduced me to a life of luxury had left his wife in his country of origin. I knew about the wife through phone call records. When he explained his situation to me, naively I believed him. I still felt deeply for him, so this was a natural reaction. I could not see myself without him. I had an inner fear of losing a man I loved.

"Where am I going to get a decent guy like him?" I asked myself. I failed to realise that anyone who cheats on his wife was as bad as all the bad people I had come across in the past. I was now conditioned to settle for second best. Eventually I naively I convinced myself that I could share this man. "Polygamy after all is not a crime in Africa," I thought. Years went by while we were together. His term of office as a diplomat ended. He left me some money to start a business. He was gone and never to be seen again.

NINE

TIME TO MOVE ON, ENOUGH IS ENOUGH

I love God when he performs miracles. I am living testimony of God's love and kindness. My life would have ended a long time ago. However, He saved me to testify to you gentle reader. I am now a healthy individual living with HIV, with nothing to worry about or fear anymore. I am with God. He saved me throughout challenging times. I was faced with troubles and tribulations, including rape, abuse, violence and low self-esteem.

Had I continued with my past life, I would have already departed from this planet. After all the abuse I experienced on the last two marriages, I would have not survived if I did not think of how to escape the troubles.

Sometimes God lets things happen, because He wants us to realise our potential. Sometimes He wants us to go through the experiences so that we can help others. Thinking of my journey now and what I went through, I can see that my strength is going to be an asset to others. The struggles made me strong and now I am able to help others.

On those check-up and treatment trips to sexual health clinics, I passed through a local hotel to have a cup of tea. I was reminiscing about my past. I was very unaware of what was going to happen in my life. I was merely holding onto scars in my heart.

I had promised myself not to love again and just concentrate on me, my health and my child. A few years went by and my concern this time was not culture or society. I wanted to put myself first. I did not even want to rush things, become laid back and not want to do anything again. Dating was out of the question. I now put my happiness first.

I then realised that I needed to do more for myself than anyone else. I started having nightmares of all my experiences. I did not know what to do anymore. A friend encouraged me to change my setting, to go abroad so I can start afresh. The idea was to go and study and become somebody. I was not sure if I could manage to live abroad at all.

Although I had friends and family scattered all over the world, I could not decide where I wanted to go. I took my time thinking of where to go and how best I could make use of what I knew before. I also considered my level of education at the time. I shelved the idea to move immediately, but I always had it at the back of my mind.

A few years later, life in Zimbabwe became tough and unbearable. Besides, the place I was living in enslaved me with memories of everything that had happened to me. I did not want to remain in the past or start any other relationship. I was now determined that I was not going to involve myself with anyone anymore. The more I stayed in the country, the more I became an outcast in the place of my birth. I knew I needed to change my life somehow. I had no idea how, but I could see myself in a better environment than the one I was used to. I had to leave so that I could offer my daughter a better life.

A Brief Life in French country

Thus far, my life had been a roller coaster. Therefore, I took my friend's advice and left Zimbabwe for another African country, looking for greener pastures. In that country, I met another man and got married to him. It was a short-lived marriage for reasons explained below. We were customarily married according to his country's traditions and values. This time, though, my parents did not get any penny because I was not home anymore.

I was a wife again, despite my conviction to never marry again.

There was a civil war talking place in my husband's country. Tribal war hit that nation hard. I was caught up in problems yet again, but different ones this time. This was a different form of violence that followed me. My husband was involved in the tribal wars. To cut a long story short, he was killed in tribal skirmishes.

This time I was very frightened, terrified, completely petrified. I had no family around. I only had my daughter (whom I had put in harm's way) and no one to run to. The language barrier was not helping either. They spoke French in that country. Although I could understand bits and pieces of the language, I was never fluent in it. People could have been plotting to kill me while I stood there with them smiling. Who knows?

Since we had started a little business with my husband, I thought I could stay and manage our business. That was not what the people of that country expected. To them I was a foreigner, period. Therefore, the business belonged to their son, not to me.

To make matters worse, I had come to their country with a child. Therefore, I did not deserve the respect that a virgin (or a childless woman) would get in that country. I did not bear a child for their son. This was considered an abomination. Therefore, I was only there to get their son's money. They made sure they tormented me with death threats. I had to leave the country with nothing, mourning the sudden death of a man I, just a few months before, had been planning my life with. This experience haunted me for a long time. For a long time, I had nightmares of the way they made me leave that country.

What I want to remind you is: "If it's not God's timing, no one will succeed in doing anything to you." I now believe that the day someone dies is written somewhere; it will not happen until God says so.

The Struggle Is Real

Now dear reader, I want you to put yourself in my shoes right now. If anyone went through my journey of life, what do you think would be happening in their life right now? I am now getting old. My body shape, the one that I had before is no more. The youthful physical beauty has gone. In addition, the flawless skin is no more! The confidence is bruised. Nowadays, men do not even look at me. I do not go out because I am always tired from work and from HIV medication that I take daily. I cannot meet anyone because men are either afraid to ask me out or think I am old. Besides, because of my age, men and women alike think I am married, so they do not make that move or ask me out on a date.

My life has never been rosy and a lot was kept in the dark. My last husband was never known to my parents. It would have been difficult for them because I was hiding the fact that I had someone. I did not bother to involve them because they would have just asked for more *lobola*. Had they known about this marriage, I am sure they would have disowned me.

I guess by doing that, I was beginning to liberate myself. I was exercising my mind and making independent choices. I never sought approval from them. In a way when he died, I blamed myself thinking maybe it was a punishment for not telling my parents about our relationship.

To be honest, I cried because once after all my problems with the last two marriages, this was really a good marriage that was abruptly interrupted by circumstances beyond my control. The fact is that I was in a hurry to get into another marriage to protect my life and my child's.

I was sad in a way, but I had to be vigilant. I would have lost my life and that of my child if I had not been with him. I still strongly think that God saved me again for the reason that He wanted me to save other women from abuse.

This just goes to tell that whenever you are faced with any kind of hardship, you should think of 'calling' God first before anyone. God is always around. He cares. He answers at his own time and we should hold on to Him. When we keep calling on Him, we will finally get help or answers.

"Thank you God the Almighty for saving me."

Journey to the Queen's Land

Being a foreigner and a widow, I had to run for my life with my child. I was now a widow for the third time. I ended up in the United Kingdom where I became a British citizen. I worked from one care agency to another. Any foreigner who has come to Britain knows how difficult it is to settle in the country. I was lucky that I began almost immediately to educate myself and learn how to adapt. After a long struggle in this new country, I was able to do finally settle down.

PART 2

TEN

1995 UNITED KINGDOM AND ITS CHALLENGES

By 1995, I was in the United Kingdom where I got sanctuary from a family member. I felt a huge weight lifted off my shoulders. Life was to prove not easy in Britain. The country has its own challenges. One has to be hard working to be able to live here.

I arrived in the UK in October. It was very warm. I could not see the difference in weather with Africa. I started thinking people were exaggerating back home that the UK was a cold place.

As we went through customs and spent some time answering a few questions, we were given temporary leave to remain which needed to be considered later. When that was finished, we walked to the train. On the train, a loud speaker announced every station we stopped at. The train was not packed like the trains back home in Africa.

What both surprised and amused me was the silence in the train. You could have heard a needle drop. Everyone in that train had their eyes glued to a free newspaper called 'The Metro'. In my mind, I thought maybe people are not allowed to talk on the train. I thought so-called 'civilised people' probably never lifted their eyes to see who was sitting next to them. Even though I was tired and hungry, I kept quiet. I was observing people and their behaviour.

The train was going at a very fast speed and I could not understand why. In my mind, I began to think we were all going to die that day. While the train was travelling at that speed, I could see some areas light up and others darken like we were entering and leaving a cave.

I could not ask anyone why it was like that. Coming from Africa, I just had to hold tight on the rails fearing for my life. I then gathered courage and asked the man sitting next to me why the train was so fast and why we had to go through the dark places and light places. The man laughed then apologised and asked me where I was coming from? I told him. He then took his time to explain to me that it was not just a normal train, but a 'tube train' that travels both underground and over-ground.

This was too complicated for me. It did not make any sense at all. A tube train? I glanced up the roof of this tube train and could not make heads or tails of what he had just explained to me. I said to myself, "One day I'll understand what a tube train is."

It took me some time to start having an understanding of British culture and society: the tube trains, the English personalities on radio and TV and the food, just to name a few. It was a great change for me, but getting used to the British way of life was just another story. I guess I need to write another book called 'Coming to Britain' to be able to explain my experience better.

Cousin or foe?

I will take the courage to explain challenges that I faced once I arrived in the United Kingdom. A cousin of mine who had agreed to accommodate me upon my arrival became 'funny' with me within a few weeks. She boycotted speaking to me saying I was only sitting at home eating and doing nothing. She said I should go and find work within two weeks of my arrival in the country.

Given everything I had gone through, this was too much pressure for me. I did not know what I needed to do in this new country and how and where to go and look for work. I was not even able to travel by myself because of fear of being lost. I did not even know my way around the place where we lived, let alone to go find work.

This added to my depression. Every night she came home from work, I had to make sure that I did not invade her space. I did not want to upset her; otherwise, she would have chucked me out. I became her housemaid, washing her uniforms and making sure I cooked nice food for her.

Anything I did, I made sure I asked her first; even taking a shower. I had to seek her permission to cook. I cleaned after her because I thought if I did not do that for her she would kick me out. This would have been disastrous for me since I was new in the country.

As time went by, a lady from next door who was babysitting for her sister became friendly with me. Every time she went to the local shops she would knock on our door and ask me if I wanted to take a walk. That lady was a Godsend.

She would take me as far as the famous Oxford Circus to show me London shops and other places. As time went by, I became comfortable enough to use buses to go around London. I now knew what tube train were and could read the tube maps without any problem. I had graduated from being a village girl to a city girl.

This girl later died. I was very devastated and had to start afresh. Up to this day, I still feel very thankful of what she did for me and I miss her dearly. It is true when they say, "Good people don't last." If it was not for this girl, who knows how much more struggle and pain I could have experienced. Soon after my friend's death my cousin told me to move out and go to find the job.

My personal journey in a cosmopolitan city started.

ELEVEN

NOT CONVINCED OF MY DESTINY

Leaving Africa, I was not sure of my destiny. I was now experiencing a life of hardship again in the Diaspora where I thought life would be better.

Life is for enjoying, and was never meant to be easy. Life is full of challenges, but who am I to dispute that? Coming to the UK was never a mistake, but it carried many risks. Challenging the challenges was the only way to go.

Through my previous experiences of life and faking it in between the years, I knew I had to continue being strong. Here I was in a strange environment with little education and no money. I had seen it all from my past life experiences. I was financially broke, but I had to put food on the table for me and my little girl to survive. I had a choice to stay illiterate and receive some income and housing benefit, or to educate myself and have a better future for me and my daughter. I had never known what it is to rely on borrowing from family and friends. I had always been independent back home. I was not going to beg in a foreign land. "My independence is my power" is the creed I lived by. I had to find out how to get a job from friends and family who had lived in Britain longer than me.

However, there was another challenge for me. I was new to the country with nothing, but the clothes on my back. The only good thing is I was allowed to work. I had also naturalised and became a British citizen.

Knowing myself and understanding my situation and background and lifestyle, I had to fight to succeed. I enrolled for a health care assistant course in 1996. I qualified and got a job as a carer, working for different nursing agencies like Montague Nurses, Aardvark Nursing Agency and Allied Health Care, to name just a few. I worked in hospitals, nursing and residential homes, domiciliary care, private hospitals, and others. This was not by choice but from a single woman's perspective, I had to survive and become independent. I could have been proud and want to start at the top. I had to be realistic about my situation and my capabilities.

I want you to understand what life is all about. Hear me out. It is not easy to be a woman and single. I used to leave home around five in the morning to catch the train to my first shift. This shift started at seven in the morning at a nursing home in Stratford, east of London. I would do a twelve-hour shift and got home at midnight.

The following morning the same routine would be repeated. I was so exhausted because of the train journeys, and having to repeat the routine for two weeks non-stop wore me out.

Doing that every day of my life was tiring, but I had no choice. I had to make a living. Thank God there were not many inspectors on the train to check tickets then. Sometimes I could not afford train fares and I resorted to dodging inspectors and travel without paying for the journey. I did not want to do this. In fact I hated who I was becoming, but that was not deliberate. I was struggling and could not afford to pay the full fare; otherwise I would have ended up not having any money for food.

The same fare dodging also happened on buses, especially on the Number 12 bus route. The route was plied by doorless buses, so I could hop on and off without paying. It was easy to be a fare dodger and make the whole journey on that bus without paying. I would pray once on the bus that I would not be caught. I did this for almost three years. I remember being caught one day when I did one of my extensions to the next tube stop. I was cautioned. At that point I knew that the habit had to stop if I still wanted to keep my respect in society.

It was easy because there was nothing like swiping the pass at the entrance, so for me those days were my lucky days as money was very short. I know some would say why not change the style of living then. It was difficult to do so. I was single and broke, yet I was the breadwinner. I had to put food on the table for me and my daughter.

Single in London, with a child

I had to figure out what do with the child I had brought into this world? It was not her fault that she did not understand why I was never home, and why I was not married. She knew her dad had died. I am sure she was asking herself all sorts of questions about her mum's singleness.

As a child, it was also difficult for her to question her mum's single life. Although in this society it is normal for a child to ask certain questions, she understood that one could not do that in my African culture. There are different values there, so she restrained herself from asking me that question.

When you are experiencing this type of life you would keep yourself to yourself, and not have much to do with many people. I did not have any friends to share the desires of my heart with.

It was fear of what people would say about me that enslaved me. It was the fact that I would be judged by society that constricted me. In my heart I knew that people would think, "Why does she not get married? Why is she working so much? Why does she not have friends or have time for her child?" I could hear these questions play in my heard all the time. I knew that people in my Diaspora community judged me. They were, after all, from Africa. However, they did not know my story. I could only console myself by working hard.

I knew I did not choose to be single, my history was long and just the thought of finding a partner with my experience was zero. I could not involve anyone in my tangled life. The truth was that life was not stopping. I had to grow and move on.

Musings

I came to England when I was only in my thirties. Time moved so much and a lot happened. I am now in my fifties, nearing my sixties.

Cher the singer was right when she said "If I Can Turn Back Time". Surely that is my wish too. Time is not waiting. I am growing old and I want to be like everyone else, but it is now too late.

Where can I begin to look for all the lost time? I was busy chasing life and survival. I also want the best in life like everyone else. This is not Africa where I could grow vegetables at the backyard of my house and feed myself and my child. There has to be a way. Which way do I go: East, South, North and West? What can I do to improve my life? As a single woman from Africa, I am in a different culture and living a different lifestyle. The only way to survival is education. I have since registered for a course in university. I am studying for a Health and Social Care degree.

The word 'love' has already faded away in my vocabulary. Finding Mr Right has proved to be difficult. I did not choose this. Circumstances are different. The situation I am in does not give room for love.

The dangers of finding love online

As we all understand getting involved with someone is another job on its own, especially with my experience. How do I get to love again? Do I have time? Do I know the person I want to go out with? Where do I meet the person supposed to be my partner? How do I create time for this love in my life? If I have to do that, I really have to be careful.

I have sometimes tried to date using internet dating sites. Oh boy! That was the worst experience I underwent. It was not good enough. I did not meet him in person. The guy wanted me to put money in his account because he claimed to be English, but working abroad on business. Online dating was new to me. This man promised me Heaven and told me all the 'sweet nothings' I last heard when I was a teenager. I said to myself, here is a chance now in Western society to get my life together.

What goes around comes round, this time again I was being played. This individual was not aware of how poor I was financially because I always present myself like I have it all and that everything is in place. He told me some sweet nothings about his job and said he had a mining company. His company had not been paid for the job they had done in Kuala Lumpur. He asked if I could lend him money to sustain himself until they were paid. I knew straightaway that it was a lie.

The thought of joining a dating site haunted me. I finally joined but usually met crocks, cheats and perverts. Not all people who join these dating sites are normal. Some have other motives besides finding love. They are manipulative. I have been fooled into thinking that I found love on any occasions. They start very well and promising the world. Some of them portray themselves as big fish, but they are not.

My experience with these dating agencies was not good. Thank God for my life experience, I am now wiser than before.

On two occasions I was made vulnerable by men of that calibre. They spent took almost three months trying to win my heart using all means possible. However, they could only come up with some story of going to work in different parts of the world. While they were there, they could only come up with some silly stories.

They would say something like, "As you know my company is a big engineering company" or tell me about something so big that I would believe they are serious in their business. They would lie about delayed cheque payments and ask for money on the pretext that they wanted to pay the labourers. They would also lie about how I was part of their future so that I would help them to continue doing their work.

One guy who claimed to be from Malaysia wrote to me, "Sweetheart, please send me £2000 or maybe £5000 so we can pay the workers." Once bitten twice shy. I vowed never to allow crooks in my life again. Not me. Not after what I had gone before. This was not going to happen again. In any case, I did not even have that amount of money in my account. I could not understand the guts of these people. How could someone ask for such an amount from me, when we had only met online? I also wondered why someone claiming to be such a big shot would be asking me for money anyway. Sometimes I simply played the game to see how far this person would go.

He promised a lot of high life which I knew was a big lie. I did not send him a penny. I just said, "Since you are in Malaysia, I have a friend who is head of the police there and is English. I will give you the address and his phone number. He can give you the three thousand pounds you need instead of sending someone to me."

He then said he did not want to meet anyone because he was very jealous. I knew then that this was a lie. He was in England and not in Malaysia. His mission was to take my money and disappear.

What he did not know was this game had been tried on me before. I did not have a penny to my name. Of course I wanted a man, but I had to vet them myself and see if they were honest. I was not a teenager anymore. Where would I find a guy and why would I go round showing him off, asking friends and family for approval? I had to do it my own way. This time around I was wiser than before.

Why do people prey on the vulnerable to fund their leisure pursuits? I was not the type of girl who could be put in that situation. Still they used other crooks to phone me and pretend to be some official. They would try to make me feel that I was in a situation that I could not come out of.

I laughed it off because they failed to get any money out of me. I was now aware of the love cheats on internet dating sites. I never trusted any such type of dating anyway, but loneliness had pushed me to the edge.

Self-deceit

Did I deceive myself all the while by pretending to be happy and content? I had come to think that I did not need anyone in my life. Repeatedly something seemed to suggest that I was not being true to myself.

When my friends saw me out there they thought I did not want to be married or I was not looking for a man hard enough. I always joked with them and say, 'When you see one out there who is not married bring him to me'. They always laughed about it.

Often they would ask me if I really wanted to put myself through the challenges of a relationship again. What they seemed to forget was that life in itself is a huge challenge. Nothing can replace companionship. Some of them thought I had everything. However, they did not realise that, in my heart, I was hurting. I did not have anything. I just smiled or laughed it off.

Sometimes I even confirmed their suspicions by saying, 'Look at me. Do you think I need a man? I have a better life than all of you married women.' It is so sad that people sometimes make these assumptions when they do not understand and do not really know what someone is going through in their life. I am writing this piece for my friends and family so that they can understand my feelings. As for the world, I would love people to stop judging people because they do not know their story.

Love is such a wonderful thing, and it is nice to be loved. I miss my husband, the father of my child. He is the only person I have ever loved. Never in a million years would I forget him. The pain of remembering has been soothed by my love for Christ. Yes, from time to time I go through challenges, but I am never alone. There is someone greater than I. Jesus Christ is saying to me, *'Come you all who are carrying a heavy burden and exchange it for a light yoke.' ... And without faith it is impossible to please him, for whoever would draw near to God must believe that he exists and that he rewards those who seek him"* (Hebrews 11 Verse 6).

I can only thank the Lord Jesus Christ for my life, for He made my way and prepared it for me. He laid greener pastures ahead of me. He gave me strength, knowledge and skills of how to deal with my situation. Thanks to the British people for accepting me and my situation, who am I to say it just happened to be accepted with my baggage.

> *"For I was hungry and you gave me food, I was thirsty and you gave me drink, I was a stranger and you welcomed me, I was naked and you clothed me, I was sick and you visited me, I was in prison and you came to me.' Then the righteous will answer him, saying, 'Lord, when did we see you hungry and feed you, or thirsty and give you drink? And when did we see you a stranger and welcome you, or naked and clothe you? And when did we see you sick or in prison you?'*
> **Mathew 25 verse: 35-45**

TWELVE

MY OWN 'LOOSE WOMAN MOMENT'

I have come to understand my situation and embrace the circumstances around it. Who am I to think it would be easy? I am single not by choice but through life experience. My situation remains a big problem to my heart.

I am not immune to love. I want to be loved, but I have no one to call my love. I am not in a relationship. The fear of my experience still keeps me from making meaningful relationships. I might have faked it all these years, and everyone thinks I am over it and do not need anyone in my life. That is a big lie.

I do wish I could meet someone and be in love again. It hurts my heart to think that I am not in love. I realise that I have to be more upfront and let people know about my feelings. Being fifty plus years old does not mean that my feelings are dead. Actually my body aches for sexual connection too. Those beautiful me moments are needed mostly at this age.

I often find myself falling apart and getting frustrated with that longing to be with someone. How can I overcome this feeling? Tough! Feelings will never go away until they are fulfilled. I might be fifty-eight but human nature forces me to find someone. Where and how do I begin fulfilling the part of me that also needs to be satisfied? I am single do not forget that girl. I can choose to ignore the feelings of wanting to be with someone or I can find a partner.

Most eligible men in my age group are married. Only a handful people are single. Statistics say women outnumber men. There are not enough men for all of us out there. Polygamy in Britain is not acceptable like in my motherland Africa.

What a punishment that my body is being refused one thing in life that could set me free. I do not have my own man. Where are the men when you need them? I have to admit though that my situation is different. I am single not by choice, but by circumstances. I am human. I also want to have sex, but I am not in a relationship.

Bisexuals, homosexuals and lesbians

I often wonder if this is the reason why some people are bisexuals, homosexuals or lesbians. This question boggles my mind all the time. Did gay and lesbian people choose to be what they are or did nature force them to be that way? Did they experience what I experienced? Whatever the reasons might be, I believe everyone needs love. There is that sense of fulfilment when you are loved.

We all have choices to make about our own lives. We have choices about who to fall in love with. It is so personal that I cannot ask anyone how he or she chooses to be what he or she is sexually. I am a believer of the Bible and its teachings. My parents made me understand that sexual relationships were only for heterosexuals. My belief was that it was to be enjoyed by two people of the opposite sex and in a relationship. That is how I chose to live my life. I am no position to judge others. Even the Bible teaches us not to judge.

I, therefore, think that everyone has a right to have sex and a right to choose a partner.

I would not judge anyone on this issue. I know how it feels. The fact remains; I am single and what do I chose to do to satisfy my body sexually is my choice. I have worked and attended my last part of my education here in Britain. I have learnt other values which I find admirable. People are open and free to discuss any topic and to express themselves. Freedom of speech was non-existent where I come from. It is not acceptable to discuss sexual behaviours unless people are attending some sort of counselling with their aunts and uncles or health authorities.

In Europe we have more access to articles in magazines and newspapers that discuss these issues. We watch films about marrying the same sex and it is not surprising. It is normal in this society. Who am I to want to make a big issue about that? Let me speak for myself. I will deal with my physical and emotional challenges the way I see fit, and I urge other independent women to do so.

When frustrated, I often find peace in the Bible. I sing and praise the Lord if I find myself in those thoughts. I pray for God's healing and love. I have to have some comfort from somewhere. I long for sex and the thoughts sometimes become too strong to bear. I am not the one who can walk to Ann Summers and buy myself a love toy. I am shy and I worry about being judged. What would I say to the cashiers? "Excuse me, how much is this rabbit and how do I use it?"

What would happen if it stops working in the middle of action? How I would know how to solve such a problem? It is not as if I am doing the normal thing. To the whole world, especially my culture it is abnormal. So reconciling these thoughts and the expectations of my culture is a constant battle. I have my African community alive and active in my life. They are my brothers and sisters away from home. I also have my church crew. What would they say if they hear about this? I also feel that God is watching me. So how do I deal with my physical, sexual emotions? These are the questions that single people are faced with, but cannot discuss.

This is physical emotion, it does not choose where and when it attacks. Anyone is bound to have such feelings, Holy or not we have to admit this and dealing with it can be very difficult. I can only say life is unfair, and being in my shoes, you do not have much choice in terms of physical emotions. This topic will be controversial to so many of my church folks but it is so secretive that they do not feel it is appropriate to discuss such an issue publicly.

I am the one experiencing this, so let none of those holy men and women judge me. I have had my own share of being judged. At least I am honest. The only person who I believe can only judge is God. This is because he sees it all. What goes on behind closed doors is no-one's business. We should all stop judging we do not know.

It is that constant struggle between the body and the brain that puts us all single people into the same category. What I know is that my body needs and desires are hard to control. I can honestly say to my fellow single people; it is only fair to find that most intimate place in your own heart and do what you can do to help yourself to escape from sexual desires. The thoughts will enslave you for a long time. Please find your own comfort and love yourself for as long as you are not hurting anyone. Let God be the judge of what you do to yourself.

I am not that old to forget about sex. Actually, I now begin to feel like I am a teenager again. So what is next? I am a Christian. They say fighting physical emotions can only work when you choose to walk with God. You can only ask God to guide you in this turmoil. You can say, "Please help me God, I am only human. These are one in a million problems of singleness. I do not want to believe that it is a curse, so what is it? I will walk with you God all the way and please show me the way."

> *"Now concerning the matters about which you wrote: "It is good for a man not to have sexual relations with a woman." But because of the temptation to sexual immorality, each man should have his own wife and each woman her own husband. The husband should give to his wife her conjugal rights, and likewise the wife to her husband. For the wife does not have authority over her own body, but the husband does. Likewise the husband does not have authority over his own body, but the wife does. Do not deprive one another, except perhaps by agreement for a limited time, that you may devote yourselves to prayer; but then come together again, so that Satan may not tempt you because of your lack of self-control. To the unmarried and the widows I say that it is good for them to remain single as I am." As said I will wait upon God* (Corinthians 7 verses: 1-40).

THIRTEEN

WHAT CAN ONE DO WHEN FAMILY DOES NOT BELIEVE YOU?

My family and relatives do not want my marriage to fail. This is because they received *lobola* from these men. None of them wants to know what happened. They all assume it was I who was wrong and are not even bothered to ask. Cultural expectations are that that the woman should endure the pain and not speak out.

To understand my situation, you have to be single. You have to walk the road that I walked. I always repeat that I do feel like being single is a curse. I have noticed this throughout my life. I am sure other single people can be witness to this. It hurts when those close to you think you are the one in the wrong always and not support you. In many people's eyes, it appears as if I chose to kill all the husbands and remain single.

Single people are looked differently if they are my age. This happens everywhere in society, for example in church, at work and in other social settings. Choosing or appointing anyone into a position of responsibility is done by looking at their marital status. Therefore, it does appear that many people do not get into positions of responsibility because they are not married.

I have learnt to live with it all my life. This is my reality. People look at me like some sort of alien. I can never freely discuss important matters, for example in church, with some of these people's husbands without getting the weird response from the wife. Sometimes I avoid conversations with certain people because of this. Women sometimes are their own worst enemy. Trust issues when you are single, are usually not there, or are of a different kind.

I find that women always suspect that I will take their husband from them. They never give me a chance. My plea in this book is to tell some of the people that I did not choose to be single. As women, we are already fighting other battles and this fight should not be necessary with me. This is not right. How do I feel about all this? I am hurting and my heart bleeds for all the people in my situation. This is because most people in my situation are not able to express themselves without the stigma that comes with it. It is frustrating.

A personal call to family and friends

This next section comes from my journal. I wrote it some time back and I think it is very poignant today as I write this book.

Just take a minute and ask yourself, "Did this person choose to be single?" I did not want this to happen to anyone or me. I want people to give me the respect that I deserve as an adult without the label that comes with being single. I want my friends to understand my feelings and emotions. A life of social rejection and hurt is not an easy one. At one point I thought this did not need to be addressed. I now realise it is one of the most difficult things single people get to experience. I am scared. I am hurt and my story haunts me sometimes.

In families, there is a lot of pressure to get married and start a family. If at my age you are not married, people have no respect for you. You are an outcast. You are a subject of mockery. To them, you are not a normal person and you do not deserve respect.

I have often noticed this at family gatherings. I am the eldest and when discussing important issues, the family does not look at my age and experience, but instead they look at my marital status. They would rather discuss family issues with my younger sister who is married than with me. Are we not supposed to have the same kind of respect? These people know me well and know all the struggles I went through in my life. They either think I am deliberately in this situation or do not understand the pressure that cultural practices impose on me.

These people have known me all my life. They are the people who charged dowry, *lobola,* during those good times when I got married. They are the people who got all the money these men were paying when I got married. Some of this money changed their lives, for example, the money paid their children's school fees. "Have they really forgotten what happened to me?" I sometimes wonder.

I know that I went through that rough patch of life. However, if they could take a minute and remember that, surely they would start treating me with respect. I was once married. I did not choose to have my husband die. Why then do I have to go through this and still suffer in silence? Is it because I got married two more times? Every marriage failed not because I wanted it that way, but circumstances did not permit me to continue with the abuse, the pain, the struggle.

I am also making a call to my family to change their attitude. I am asking them to reflect on the pain some of the things they did and still do cause in my life. I am asking them to change and accept me as I am. They are the very people who should understand my situation. I am human. I have feelings. I wish they could think again. I did not want this to happen to me, and I think they should be there to support and respect me because they know my story. I am still the same person from the beginning up to now, so I expect them to give me respect and we can be in a better relationship with each other.

Sometimes I wonder why I feel so lonely. For me, understanding and embracing my situation has somehow made me strong and be able to take things lightly so that I do not hurt my feelings. I have learnt to accept how people and the public perceive me. Even in church situations, they discriminate against me. People think twice before they appoint someone who is single to perform certain church duties. I have to carry myself in a certain way so that I fit in with the rest of the people and get respect. I cannot be free and choose to be me because of fear of rejection.

In a way, I feel society emotionally abuses me and people do not realise their biases and their prejudices in dealing with me. It is very easy to be judged and labelled when you are single. It is painful to realise that people who knew me when I was young do not respect me and find me to be an outcast.

Why do I seek approval from strangers if my own family do not remember my story? It is embarrassing and disheartening at the same time. I urge my family to remember next time when they are talking to me that I have feelings too. I am human. I did not choose to be in this situation. I only hope that God will keep their lives straight and that they will never find themselves in my situation.

Life is for living. Do you really know how painful and hurtful this is to me? I have lost all my confidence. I find myself having low self-esteem. People who are supposed to know better and understand my circumstances do not. I have to think twice before I join them in any conversation. I am considered not worthy.

Why does it have to be like that? I only hope and pray that my family, friends and relatives and their children will never have a story like mine. God makes us all. The love of God should make us unite and not dislike each other. We are brothers and sisters, and let us love each other before we love other people out there. Charity begins at home.

I hope we all have learnt a lesson on this. If I was a younger person, maybe I would have taken my life; but somehow I found strength in my story. It is never too late to change. Please accept me as your big sister again. I did not choose the circumstances.

It appears to me I am the black sheep of the family. I am still the same person. The only difference is my life has never been one straight line. I did not choose it, but that is how it is. Those who ill-treat me because of my marriage status or disrespect me should find it in their hearts to understand my struggles.

What is family for if you cannot love one another? I love my family dearly and not even a day goes by without me praying for all of my family members. I believe this is not going to offend anyone, all my loved ones, but it has to be said sometimes. Those who did not know the impact of their prejudices now do. Therefore, I hope they realise that they can learn from their mistakes. It is hurting me, it is hurting my soul and it is paining me. I love my family sincerely. I always wish them love, peace and happiness.

To my fellow colleagues, society and those people who believe single people are of less value, you do have a lot to learn. Let us accept and embrace every human being the way they are. Until you know his or her story, you have no right to judge anyone. I will never judge whom I do not know.

Getting married was only luck and that does not give anyone the right to comment on anyone's life. You are not in their shoes. The question I keep asking myself is, "Am I cursed" or "Why would people keep throwing all the rubbish at me?" I did not choose to be single. I deserve to be treated with respect and love.

I am a human being and I have feelings, and do not deserve the hurt and the pain. I go through some tough times just from everyday life. Fighting family and friends' prejudices and judgement only serves to add insult to injury. I am already vulnerable and I need kindness and understanding.

I choose to be quiet when I am attacked; but this is only for the sake of peace. I know I have my own reasons why I do not want to fight back. I try to respect everyone so why can't I be respected too.

I urge my family, friends, and anyone who has not thought about these issues to change their ways for better relationships. We can than all live happily. If I could turn back the hands of time, I could do better. However, I am old now. It looks like some things are better left alone. Let us live in harmony and be one, whether we are single, married, gay, lesbian, black or white. We are all human. Let us love and respect one another and make this world a better place. Remember what goes around comes around. You do not know what God has in place for you. It is right to do good always.

"To the choirmaster: according to The Doe of the Dawn. A Psalm of David. My God, my God, why have you forsaken me? Why are you so far from saving me, from the words of my groaning? O my God, I cry by day, but you do not answer, and by night, but I find no rest. Yet you are holy, enthroned on the praises of Israel. In you our fathers trusted; they trusted, and you delivered them. To you they cried and were rescued; in you they trusted and were not put to shame. .." **Psalm22 verses 1-31**

FOURTEEN

ABUSE CHANGED ME

It has never been easy for me to find friendship and maintain it. I would love to keep all the people I come across as friends or acquaintances. I often ask myself why they all drift away from my life.

At first, I failed to realise that my own life was a mess. That made me suspicious of people and their intentions. I often did not give anyone a chance to love me as a human being. I have spent all my life trying to cope with rejection and that alone can cause mental torture. It can create and perpetuate broken relationships. It can become a self-fulfilling prophecy that people are inherently bad.

None of my friends understand why I am the way I am. I now see the roots of my behaviour as a blockage to myself and to others. I have driven everyone apart. I wish I could turn back the hands of time and restart life with the experience and knowledge of life that I now have. I can only apologise to those close friends and family I have hurt in my lonely life.

Singleness is really a sad life. Because of my experience, I still struggle to trust anyone. That is somehow sad, but that is how I see it. I did not choose to be in it nor did I understand what this would do to my future. After abuse at a young age, life was always going to be a difficult and uphill struggle. Surely, if during my childhood there were advocates and social services, maybe an intervention would have saved me from the pain I endured. Help came later in my life, but not late.

I am not a bad person if you get to know me. I have had close friends in my life. However, many times before they know me that well, I say some things that upset them. I never see them again. This is not deliberate. They get upset, nevertheless. Then they leave and I am back to Square One.

It is not a question of how I say things to anyone. It is the way I sometimes feel, and it feels like the right correct way to protect my inner feelings. I somehow feel that is the only way I can fight my battles and no one can take advantage of me. I become defensive. By saying only one bad word, I can destroy a good friendship and never see that person again.

I really try to save my relationships with people, but it sometimes happens anyway. I am work in progress. I try my best to do better all the time. Finding love and maintaining it is hard. I have found a remedy though and I feel it is not too late. God!

Most of the people I have had meaningful relationships with in my life have gone. They have moved on without me. I find comfort in the words of some pastors like United States pastor, T.D. Jakes. When he preaches, I find comfort in his words. For example, one of his famous sayings is *"If they go, let them go. Maybe it was never meant to be anyway"*. When I listen to such words, I feel like I am not alone in this battle. I feel that at least someone knows and understands my story, even if they have never met me before.

When friends disappear from my life, I feel the pain and anguish. In some cases, I am not the only one to blame, so I forget and move on. Sometimes this comes across as arrogance. It is not. I am who I am because of my circumstances. I know it is my experience that made me not trust anyone. It is something I struggle with every day and would need to do my best to rebuild that trust.

I have lived with myself and carried this for at least fifty-eight years. My wish is to strive for a better me and better things. I have realised that I had a sad life, not because I had bad parenting, but because of what I went through. My experiences put me in this situation. Day in, day out, I fight my emotions and feelings; but the goal is to be a better me and have better relationships in my life.

I have accepted my way of life and seem to find ways of dealing with how I am perceived. It is not an easy life, but I will live with it and try every single day to change it. True friends will accept me and understand my life. I have lived with it and I will try my level best to change the situation through my own behaviour. I always pray, "Help me God. I want to be great woman."

I believe that it is never too late to change. I have come a long way from being uneducated to being educated. I have come across many challenges and find ways to deal with them in my time, and in my own way. I have overcome a lot of things and as a single person. Controversial and challenging decisions had to be made.

Good or bad, my life moved on. Nothing that comes my way surprises me anymore. I still have to deal with it as a single individual. I know that whatever I do in life, I must always have a vision. It is what organises my life, drives my ambition and allows me to live a fulfilling life. I am a changed woman. I have found Christ and I am happy. I cannot change my past, but I love to make friends and keep them. I am as positive as I have ever been.

I thank God that I am able to help others in their own situations or in situations similar to mine. I am a counsellor, an aunt, a big sister, and a true agony aunt to those who are abused and less fortunate in life. I now work as a volunteer with charity organisation: Save the Children of Africa and Widows of Warren Park D.

I have raised funds and helped to make life better for others. I will go back to Africa one day and help those vulnerable children experiencing what I went through. I want to give back to society and build this world to make it a better place. Nevertheless, the struggle is very real despite all this. I have to fight the prejudices and the social norms that made my life a living hell. My aim is to make sure every child has a voice and a vision.

Every child should have a voice and be heard. I do not wish any child to go through it alone, as I did in my own situation. God has freed me from anger, hatred and deceit. For that, I will forever be thankful. We must protect children. My own situation should never be the experience of another child. Life should be for living and enjoying.

Name-calling and abuse is the life that I grew up knowing. I will never let anyone face abuse in his or her life. I now dedicate my life to making sure that no one is abused again. Making friendships should be easier now that I have addressed by my own sadness and the root of it. I now have thousands of friends and a lot more connections on social media.

It is only difficult to start speaking. However, I advise anyone going through my story to seek help before it is too late.

"He who dwells in the shelter of the Most High will abide in the shadow of the Almighty. I will say to the Lord, "My refuge and my fortress, my God, in whom I trust." For he will deliver you from the snare of the fowler and from the deadly pestilence. He will cover you with his opinions, and under his wings you will find refuge; his faithfulness is a shield and buckler. You will not fear the terror of the night, nor the arrow that flies by day." **Psalm 91 Verses 1-6**

FIFTEEN

CAN A MARRIED WOMAN CLAIM RAPE FROM HER HUSBAND?

As far as my culture is concerned, there is no such thing as rape when you are married. It is expected that you do not challenge your husband when he 'demands' sex. Sex is part of marriage. We are expected to provide sex to the husband when he wants it. This is a passport to physical abuse. Women do not report this to anyone because it is unheard of for a woman to refuse conjugal rights to her husband.

If a married woman refuses to have sex with her husband, it becomes a family issue. Aunts and uncles who married the bride off would intervene. As I grow older and after have gone through the ordeal of abuse and the nasty experience of marrying my tormentors, I have nightmares when I think of getting married again. Another part of me would like to get married. I face this contradiction.

It is unfortunate that in my time such issues were not up for debate. I was expected to endure the pain of abuse that married life brought. This caused a lot of pain in my life. This brought a lot of shame to me.

For thirty years, after all these failed marriages, I never opened up to anyone until I became hospitalised due to high blood pressure. I went to Princess Elizabeth Hospital in Essex in 2013. I could not understand what was going on in my life. I only remember being scared, but could not tell that the impact of the scars would last long.

I urge all parents to continue speaking to their children so that they can understand their feelings. In my case, it was expected that I could not be the first one to speak out. I grew up in the 1960s and we were expected to be quiet. We kept many secrets. It was expected that a 'good child' from a 'good family' would not question social and cultural norms.

I wish I had known the impact of those secrets. However, how would I have known? If I had a choice, I would not have kept any secrets at all. My struggle was made worse by the fact that I had many health issues to deal with which were caused by those marriages. This was too much pressure to withstand. Although I tried ignoring everything, I could not heal my heavy heart. I was overwhelmed by traumas of the past. I was bleeding from the inside. The scars left by pain and suffering still have an impact to me.

Can anyone tell me there is no God out there? I have lived as an HIV positive woman for over thirty years after abusive marriages. Even though I contracted this illness, I am still standing today. To me that is a testament to the existence of God.

I quickly understood that being HIV positive and accepting my condition made me strong from the outside. However, I needed to deal with the inside turmoil as well. This depressed me and raised my blood pressure. The doctors at Princess Elizabeth Hospital were exceptional. They helped me a lot and for me not to mention them or thank them would be a bad example of not showing gratitude. I would have had stroke then because my blood pressure was soaring.

I do not remember how many times I was picked up by ambulance after collapsing on the streets. I recall one occasion when someone jumped into the road to stop cars from driving over me after I collapsed in the middle of the road. This was in a place called Camberwell Green, in South East London in the United Kingdom. I was quickly picked by ambulance and taken back to Kings College Hospital which I had just left ten minutes earlier. I believe that I was saved from death, so that I can testify to the power of God's grace. I was saved to testify.

After this incident, the nursing staff never allowed me to leave my bed. I was given a bedpan and commode to help me with toileting. Nurses were washing me in bed, so I would not walk to the bathroom. They feared I would fall and stroke again. I thank the staff and all the cleaners who were exceptionally phenomenal.

As if it was not enough, my weight was piling up. At the beginning of this book, I mentioned that I was eating for comfort. I did not want people to notice that I had become thin because of ill health. I did not want to grow thin and ill. I would have suffered stigmatisation. In the 1980s, people would have run away from me if they had known I had HIV. Life was hard enough for people with chronic diseases like mine.

From my own story, I learnt not to judge people until I know their story. I can offer wise counsel, but only after understanding where they are coming from and what their story is. If all people could take time to understand other people's stories, we would live a life that is loving, caring and fulfilling. I have taught my grandchildren to love everyone, regardless of their health condition, colour, creed or their background. I strongly believe this is what parents should teach their children.

I thank the Lord for the wisdom He imparted to me. That wisdom has prompted me to write my own story. However, in my first books, I tried to tell my story as frankly as possible; but I always felt that I sometimes self-censored because I was constrained by the fear that my family would desert me. I was anxious. I was not sure how people would react to what I said in my writings. In these later books, I found my voice. I do not fear anyone or anything. All I want is for people to understand the pain caused by my marriages. Thirty years is a long time to face abuse.

I urge all parents to listen to their children even if society and culture pushes them into marriage. They should try to find out if they are happy in that marriage now and again, for there might be in big trouble and they may be silently facing many problems in future.

SIXTEEN

PSYCHOLOGICAL THOUGHTS THAT COME WITH DOMESTIC VIOLENCE

I have often heard people say that I fake my illness. It is easy for people to say that because they do not understand me and never take time to do so. Those who have never travelled your road or suffered a single day of what you had to endure do not understand your story. Many people would speak behind my back and judge me without having any evidence of what they were saying. It hurts so much and it makes it difficult to try to explain to those people how it feels to hear things said about you.

The road has been bumpy. It gets rough when people are not accepting each other's situations. For someone with a chronic disease, the suffering increases. The condition becomes very difficult to cope with, especially when you know that other people are getting joy out of your suffering. I have experienced many instances where people find joy in hurting me. However, I have always tried to take it on the chin and move on.

The experience of domestic violence, abuse and rape makes one lose all confidence. For me, self-esteem went out of the window. Nevertheless, I rose up and started telling my story. I realised that speaking to others and empowering women, helped my wounds to heal. It has been the toughest thirty years of my life, but indeed this is the "light at the end of the tunnel". The struggles are there, but they are not like those of the last thirty years.

The psychological torture one endures through keeping their illness a secret makes that illness worse. I was always anxious and nervous when faced with everyday life situations. I struggled with many day-to-day things; things that others would accomplish within a short time. For example, I had poor memory, flashes of anger and many mood swings. I spent a lot of time trying pretending to be someone else so that I could fit in. It was very hard to lead such a double life. I was always afraid that people would know my secret.

The thing about keeping a secret is that you have to keep remembering what you lie about so that you do not confuse those you lied to. Another reason is that you will end up making a fool of yourself. Imagine keeping up appearances with a baggage full of lies behind you. I took up challenges which I definitely know that with my health I cannot perform them. I was trying to fit in and prove to people that I could do this even when I was at the lowest point in my health.

I have probably deceived myself by taking difficult courses knowing that my memory is poor. Although I made it through most of the courses, it was a struggle. I did not cope well. I went through a lot of pain, but eventually I succeeded.

Controlling my temper has been the hardest thing to cope with. I should confess that people find me rude or arrogant. That is all to do with the life of medication that I live. Many people would not understand, but I do. Having to live a life of tablets for over thirty years was always bound to cause some reaction at some point. The reaction causes problems that alienate you from people, from those you love.

Sometimes I promise things that I will not fulfil only to please others. I am generous by nature and I find it hard to say no to people. At one time, it became so bad that I gave a friend some money and failed to pay my own rent. I now understand that this has to do with that desire to be loved, to belong and to be appreciated.

Once I realised my insecurities, I stopped trying to please people. This caused problems with people who had come to expect things from me. Many of them have drifted away since they knew I was not generous anymore. I could not do it anymore. I was struggling with my own problems.

As for friends, they are supportive of my condition. We joke and laugh about everything. In fact, I look at my HIV condition and view it as just a diagnosis by the doctors, but nothing that will stop me from doing anything I put my mind to. I take my tablets daily and I do not recall being sick or hospitalised for over a long time. I am so used to it that at times I even forget I have an incurable disease. I have accepted my condition positively and so has everyone around me. I do not expose myself to things that I know are not good for my health.

I keep healthy by regularly visiting the gym, eating healthy, keeping myself warm all the time, avoiding stressful situations that pull me down. I know quickly when things are not right and address them immediately.

It is a psychological battle all the time to make some serious decisions. I question my decisions many times and I doubt myself. I never act on my first impulses and many times, I ask for my daughter's opinion or help me with decision-making. I also have bouts of anger. Anger has been an issue for me most of the times. It was anger and denial that made me delay taking my medication.

I keep praying that I will not lose my memory to mental health problems like dementia. Sometimes I am very forgetful and I worry that there may be a link between HIV and the memory loss. However, this is not about me. It is about the role that I have assigned for myself: to help other people. I am very careful in everything I do and avoid doing things that present a danger to others.

During the early days of my HIV diagnosis, I was thinking of taking my own life. I was suicidal because I lacked knowledge and awareness of the condition. I was concentrating more on the embarrassment I would face if people found out. It was my perception.

That is now history. I have moved on and everything is as fine as it could be, given my circumstances. I do forget things sometimes. I am only human. Today I enjoy my life and know that I have lived long because of my attitude towards my HIV diagnosis. I can still go on with my business. I am happy that the illness makes me keep track of my life and check on myself now and again. This helps deal with other help issues which I would not have dealt with if I did not have the condition. Regular check-ups keep me healthy. The regular blood tests allow the doctors to monitor any irregularities that may arise.

I am glad I am in charge of my life now. There is nothing to worry about in terms of my health. All is okay for me to live a clean life and not mixing myself with people who may infect me. I look after myself always.

SEVENTEEN

A JOURNEY WITH HIV MEDICATION

It has not been easy at all, but I have to be honest about my own life. I have lived a life which I never expected to live, after all the troubles I went through. I really thank the Almighty God for keeping me alive. The life of pills is not a joke. I have survived for thirty-two years since my diagnosing, gulping tablets throughout those years.

I am happy I am alive. However, I have to be strong for my grandchildren whom God has given me. I never thought I would be alive to witness my first grandchild being born, finishing secondary school and now going to Upper Sixth or Year 13, then to University afterwards. God gave me another grandchild. I am thankful to Him.

I left Zimbabwe in denial about my status. I never believed in the diagnosis from home. When I came to Britain, I did not do anything about the condition and started working. I measured my health with the weight I was carrying. I naively thought it was a misdiagnosis and that I was healthy and strong.

I kept the diagnosis in a secret place in my heart and never wanted to discuss it with anyone. However, my body was wearing out. I was getting ill and going towards a dead end.

A turning point came in 1997. I was just going on with my business as usual. I was overweight. My journey without medication was ending. As I was coming from work, I collapsed without knowing what was going on with me. I was picked by ambulance and taken to Whitechapel Hospital in East London. They carried out blood tests.

When they realised that my address was from South East London, they offered to transfer me to Kings College Hospital which was nearer my home. I agreed. At least I was near home. A few days later, the results of blood tests came. I was to get the shock of my life. I was HIV positive!

I was offered counselling. My journey with tablets again started in Britain. I was made aware of my viral load which was very fatal and the doctors told me that I was lucky to be alive because my immune system was compromised and my body was unable to cope. It was weak.

Unbeknown to me, I thought I was health because of my weight. I was deceiving myself. They administered medication which had many side effects on me. I struggled again with side effects caused by medication. I had to get the medication changed. The doctors tried different types of medication until they got the right one. With the side effects gone, the improvement on my body was vast. I began to feel very strong. I had more energy than before and wanted to do more activities. I even enrolled at the local gym and started swimming after the doctor's recommendation.

I become more active. I started going out more, meeting more people and I even went back to college to study. After few months, I had made a lot of improvement in my health. Doctors commended my speedy comeback. I moved myself from denial to reality and medication did not give me any side effects.

Amazingly, today I can speak to my friends about my condition. When I tell them my story, they all cannot believe me. Even if I show them the medication, they still cannot believe me. I joke about my illness. I tell my friends that acceptance of my situation has made it so easy for me to get along and do anything in life.

I do not worry anymore about medication. Swallowing the HIV tablets, especially the big and tasteless ones, is not that much of a problem now. All I get is some colouring of my tongue and my mouth, but that is easy to live with. I swallow these tablets daily like any other food. I do not feel that it is medication. That has made me live an active, stress-free and positive life.

All I worry about now is missing my daily intake of tablets. I keep going, as life has to be lived. I am a happy individual and those tormentors who gave me this illness do not affect me anymore. I just wish they would know that I am in a happy place. Ironically, their own life has ended. Mine was not shortened. I will not let their ignorance affect me. I wish them well wherever they are. God help them.

I urge any teenager to be careful and be tested for HIV/AIDS before they start any sexual relationship. It is important that they are tested. They must use condoms to be safe. This is the only way they will live a better life than I did. "A healthy life for a health relationship," is the creed by which they should live. Let us all be careful. I hope they will take my advice seriously because the journey that I travelled is not easy.

Not all days will be good if you are HIV positive. Sometimes your viral load is low and the immune system becomes weak. Sometimes energy goes out of the window and the willingness to do things becomes zero. There is an emotional side to it as well. Anger grows on you sometimes when you think about what happened. This lowers your self-esteem. It is a type of depression and sometimes you feel you are unable to cope. During these low episodes, people will not understand you. You sometimes hate yourself, blame yourself and not like the person that you are and that you have become. Just take care and be careful.

Missing doses of medication is not advisable at all. This can easily bring back some weaknesses to the body. As soon as you remember that you forgot the medication, make sure you take it immediately. You can then make up for the time difference by slowing down on the other medication.

Medication dreading has become the thing of the past for me. I do not hesitate to take my medication anymore. I am now used to taking it. Had I not been taking my medication as expected, I might not have been here.

It is of paramount importance to continue taking medication as described by doctors so as not to trigger other problems. I am happy that the doctors finally got the right tablets for me. There are no more side effects and no reactions. As long as I live, tablets will be an everyday thing. I live this life. I am happy. There are no more concerns about why I contracted HIV. I am glad all is going well with medication. However, even though the viral load remains undetectable taking medication is a non-stop cycle.

EIGHTEEN

IS THER LIFE AFTER DOMESTIC VIOLENCE?

My experience did a lot of harm in my life. I think this is expected. Anyone who has had a life like mine is bound to be challenged at every stage in his or her life. I thank those people who have shown me the other side of life which I thought I could not experience at all.

I have lived my life feeling incomplete all the time since my HIV diagnosis. By this, I mean I have never experienced a true way of living. I have never really been in love. I have to imagine all the time what true love is.

I have suffered from lack of confidence although in front of people I put on a brave face. I put on an act. I pretend to be very confident, but I am not. Besides, this being a result of my medical condition, it is also a product of my strict upbringing. When I was young, children were beaten up by their parents for every little mistake they did. We all grew up timid and in fear. This took a huge toll on our confidence and our self-esteem.

My generation grew up during the colonial period. There was conflict during the war years, the fight for independence. Growing up in the country, girls were abused by soldiers during the war. We provided 'company and comfort' to the soldiers while we were children. When I think deeply about this, I realise that we never had an easy life after all. I grew up with very low self-esteem and lack of trust. Sometimes my insecurities come back to haunt me. I do not really want to get very close to anyone due to fear of being deceived. Who can blame me for this?

I struggle most of the time to trust people. It does not matter how close this other person is, at the back of my mind, I would still think they are not genuine. If it is friendship, I still look deep into their heart to try to understand if they have a motive or not. As for men, love and dating, I'm still not convinced there is such a thing called love I am always looking after me first, thinking that in every relationship I go into I will end up being hurt.

Although I have tried counselling and coming to terms with my traumatic experience, changing and learning to trust people will take a lifetime. I am very strong and I love helping others. However, I have to change my mind set to be able to trust and love again. I always think of looking after Number One first.

I motivate, counsel and teach others about forgiveness and how to get bad experiences out of your mind. I am surprised that those people I help come back and thank me for having set them in the right path. That probably is a gift I have, of helping others better than I help myself. What I struggle with is that doubt; that little voice of negativity inside me. I need to exorcise that voice. It needs to come out and all things would be clear. I should be able to do this because the worst part of my life is long over. It has been experienced and done with.

Yet I soldier on daily. I use prayer most of the time to forgive myself. I try to live a normal life always. If only I could trust and not believe that there is certain things I cannot do because of age, then nothing would ever happen to me again.

I still dream of the abuse and the way all my life has been even though I know I am safe. I still have nightmares. Surely, there is a correlation between the psychological impact we experience and our emotions. Professionals play an important part. However, the rest of us are left to do most of the work to make sure our souls are healed.

It has been a journey for me and with prayers, I am getting there. I have reached a point where I ignore all the sad moments and concentrate on the best times in order to be happy.
This is wisdom for me. I will keep praying and forgiving all the people who abused me and messed up my life. God has already done his part on them. I believe they lived a short life because of their sins.

This has led me to repent and know that God decides our destiny and not us. The men who abused me are all dead. They gave me an illness, but God found it worthy to keep me alive and repair my life after they had made my life a living hell.

As to the young ones who are experiencing violence or domestic abuse in their marriage, I would urge them to get out abusive marriages. There is no excuse for abuse. They should not stay in those abusive relationships as I did in the hope that things would change. The only change I saw was to be infected with a chronic disease.

I turned to God. Nothing on this earth is permanent. We all die but we die in different ways and at different times. Some people die of natural causes, some die from car accidents, but if you have not done any bad thing to anyone and know only God, you will be saved. I thank God even though I have been infected with HIV. Otherwise, I am a healthy person and my only health concern has been high blood pressure. My eating too much to cover my loss of weight exacerbated this illness. I did not want people knowing that I was ill. If I had lost weight, they would have suspected that something was wrong.

I have an excellent life. I have never been in hospital again because of a poor immune system. Since I knew my diagnosis, I have lived a cleaner and healthier life. I hope that my story will help others to avoid falling victim to people who will abuse them.

Young women especially, should be careful of meeting the wrong people. They should be tested. In terms of relationships, they should not settle for mediocrity. They should know that they are loved and that their life is worth more than material possessions. I say to them: *"Eat well, exercise more and hang around with positive people who help you. Also, do not forget to laugh and not take life too seriously. Please take care of yourself. You only live once. Please leave a legacy that is admired by people."*

NINETEEN

IS DOMESTIC VIOLENCE A SIGN OF WEAKNESS OR BULLYING?

People who abuse others have certain insecurities that we do not know about. They abuse others to fill the gap left by those insecurities. They abuse others to feel good about themselves. We often think that we are guarding ourselves from whatever is happening around us. What we need to know is how to heal, so we do not have such insecurities ourselves; otherwise the cycle of abuse will not be broken.

If we dig deep and examine ourselves, we would know exactly what needs to be fixed within us. As for abusers, they might not even know themselves well. They may not be aware of the circumstances that made them the way they are. They might choose to ignore something that is crucial in their life that needs attention or treatment. An awareness of their circumstances is very important. This intervention is very important and can be done effectively through therapy.

Looking back at my own experience, I realise that my second and third husbands needed to examine their lives closely to find out what had caused so much pain in them so much that they had to make the lives of other people a living hell. They needed to pay attention to their own lives first before marrying anyone.

They both grew up in poverty. Poverty was a major cause of many of the issues they were dealing with in their adult lives. They both had no father figure, so they lacked a male role model. This lack of a father figure in their lives meant that they had no one to discipline them or teach them proper family values. They needed proper guidance on how to build a family. Love is one of the most important pillars of a strong family. My second and third husbands lacked this important pillar. They lack emotional intelligence.

When those basic but important pillars are missing from an early age, how can we expect miracles in later life? Children need role models they can learn from, emulate so that they understand the right way of doing things, and know how to treat others. Loss of family members, especially those that are supposed to take care of us, creates an emotional gap that is very difficult to fill. Children end up learning important things from outside the family setting. It is not sufficient to teach them only how to love. They should know the value of relationships.

Domestic violence and domestic abuse break relationships. Broken relationships lead to broken family structures. The children who grow up in these broken families are often the ones who hurt others in later life. This creates a cycle of violence which has to be broken through some professional intervention.

In the United Kingdom, there is an extra layer of problems apart from broken relationships. Substance abuse is that layer. Children who grow up in families where there is substance abuse also have major problems developing relationships in later life. Although I came from a well-off family with great parenting, my father abused my mother in many ways. I can vividly remember moments that amounted to abuse. Although she was well educated, I guess that culture constrained her or stopped her from taking action.

I witnessed situations where my mother was being beaten for petty things. Many times, she was blamed for things that we did as children, things that she would not have been able to stop anyway. We were just kids getting slightly mischievous, as children do. Seeing my mother beat up put a lot of pressure on me as a child, pressure that the parents were not aware of. I grew up scared of what might happen to me as a woman. I saw men differently.

Many times, I saw my mother being bullied and made to feel so little in front of us, the children. We could not do anything to stop the violence. We were not allowed to speak or to answer back. I have had some time to reflect on this abuse. It is only now that I realise that my father's upbringing was a contributory factor to his abusive behaviour.

Watching it from a distance, I can see some of my family members not being able to cope with their own lives until they get professional help. Life, for some of my family members, is just like a vicious circle and as the old adage says, 'What goes round comes round'. Most people who violate other people's lives in most cases are hurting inside. The reason why might not even be known to them.

I now think of domestic violence as a sign of weakness. Either the abuser knows this type of weakness or the abuser is unaware of where his hate is coming from. How then is abuse a weakness on the part of the abuser? It is by failing to admit that there is something within oneself that needs immediate attention. It would be important to address it once one knows that there is a problem.

If pain and bad upbringing are not addressed and are allowed to continue without being taken control of, they grow some roots within an individual. It then changes the way they see things or value life. The lack of emotional intelligence makes caring for someone would very difficult. If you fail to understand your problems and address them, how can you be able to understand other people's problems or care for them?

After my research and my own experience with the men I married, I have started to understand how people's lives and backgrounds and how their impact other people's lives. I realised that my ex-husbands' behaviour towards me was influenced by the way they were raised. Once I realised this, I then accepted it as inevitability on their part. The issue became even clearer when I realised that we had such challenges in my own family.

I now believe that poverty experienced during the time of growth sometimes leads to many challenges in later life. We often have bad life experiences if we have no role models to inspire us and teach us important things about relationships and about life in general. We cannot expect two live wires to work together without causing a big destruction.

Past trauma leads to abuse, violence and rape. Parents should be mindful of how they raise their children. They should make sure they support their children all the way by loving and caring for them. One day these children could become good citizens and treat other people with love and respect.

TWENTY

ONLY HOPE AND FAITH KEPT ME GOING

The fact that I am well and alive to tell my story is a miracle, but it is also a question of hope. It is hope that kept me going. Had I not sought Christ in all my troubles, my trials and my tribulations, this disease would have taken my life a long time ago. I had to fight my emotions as well as my physical challenges in order to come out of this mess. I had no confidence in myself. I thought staying married would have made me whole. I was searching in the wrong place.

I should have left these marriages sooner. This should have happened before I was in the mess that I ended up in. Trust was lacking and I thought I could not manage at all by myself.

Embracing Christianity helped me a lot in the end. I was then able to have faith in my future. Although I was already ill, I hoped that my life would be better off without the men who had caused so much grief and pain in my life. Having to be made a slave by someone I trusted and loved, my husband, did so much damage to my emotions and to my health.

I remember those days I could never imagine my life would change at all. However, I had to be bold and visualise another possibility, another life. This was only possible if I left these marriages. I only held on to them because I still had that mentality of being a well behaved first-born child. I was expected to be exemplary. That often meant keeping quiet, staying married and humble.

I was raised to think that divorce would make me a big sinner, although I asked myself several times what marriage was all about. I always knew if I stayed in the type of marriage I was in, I would never be happy in my life. For the first time I prayed to God to forgive me and to give me good reasons for getting a divorce. I was desperate to get out the marriage, but society and culture were keeping me in an institution I was not happy to be in.

One I had found God, I then started looking at things in a positive way. I was thinking of how I would find a better job and look after my child. Even though I was able to take care of my daughter and myself on a city council salary, I still believed that I would change my situation one day once I was alone.

I guess God had seen me struggling then made this last husband pack his stuff while I was away and left. I trusted and believed dearly that the exit of my husband was a gift from God. My faith had pushed the enemy away and I had been given an opportunity to start my life all over again. It was a huge relief that he had left. I was now left with my daughter and no extra mouth to feed or to worry about. Things started working in my favour from that time onwards. All those dreams and thoughts of doing well were now looking real. I had been given a new lease of life and I was not going to misuse it.

What I know is God will never fail us if we can only have faith and trust in Him. For me, it was dreams come true. I had to believe that no situation becomes permanent unless God says so. All my hopes and dreams of leaving my motherland and going far away were fulfilled.

I wish all people could seek guidance from God when they are faced with troubles. God hears our cry and He answers at his own pace. Dreams come true only if people could remain faithful and hopeful.

When one is a child of God, they do not need to work so hard to get the results they want. However, God looks after His own people. He rewards His own even when they are caught up in a storm. Had I not been patient, I would have miscalculated the whole move by taking my life.

We should clear our minds and understand that we should work according to God's promises. The highest level of working is being able to help others meet their needs and love them. As children of the Highest God, we have a clear understanding of our position in society.

As we all know, God never fails us. He is always around to protect us no matter what's thrown at us (*Psalms, 41*). I know inwardly that God is always around and He will never leave me or forsake me. As His child, He was preparing me to save others by making me go through these challenges and learning how to overcome them.

I now understand that the first area of investment in God's Kingdom is to strive and help our young ones. They should not have misleading leadership. What I know is that my experience was not only for me, but also for sharing with others. God is happy with people who share and consider other people's needs. It is an honour to trust His word so we can influence the lives of others.

The struggles I went through meant that I had to stand straight to overcome them. I had to stand up like the Biblical Esther and face whatever was thrown at me. Therefore, I see my role as to be able to impact the next generation of young women. I am happy under the present circumstances. I am now able to enlighten other young women of what could happen if they get involved in wrong and ungodly relationships.

Living my life like the Biblical Esther's in this storm helped me not to make wrong decisions. Although I struggled in many ways and endured the pain, I honestly believe that one day this would happen. They say, "God rewards those who wait". This axiom became a reality to me. The pain of my experience was turned into peace, purpose and power. I always refer to these three Ps and they are important in my life. Remember when Israel was in need, people stood up to help? So why would we stay without seeking help? It is about time we take charge of our lives.

I will always be there to work with those in need. The passion of helping others comes to me naturally as a mother. I have a responsibility to speak to young girls and boys to help them so they do not follow a road like mine which was scary and bumpy.

TWENTY ONE

R.I.P. MOTHER

I always have this personal conversation: "Poor mother what killed you? We all thought it was cancer. Why then were you always groaning complaining that your arm was hurting? R.I.P. Mwenewazvo. No one will ever know exactly what happened to you."

When I think about how my mother endured pain in her domestic situation, I ask myself many questions. I hope it was not the pain and emotions of the storm that she went through that took her life. Although the doctors gave us a diagnosis, the only truth was known by her. A big number of women in Africa die from domestic violence and abuse especially those in my generation and beyond. Could this have been my mother's fate as well?

The doctors gave us a diagnosis. The truth was known by her. We trust it was that 'truth' that took her away from us. A big number of women in Africa die from domestic violence and abuse, especially those in my generation and beyond.

African women, especially those of my generation and beyond, endure a lot of pain. Men lead the family as breadwinners and they take a lot of joy being in control.

Once they get married, the women are considered as a chattel, as property in the house. That characterisation of women gives men the authority to do as they please without any consent. I think *lobola* should not be charged in a way that appears as if the family is selling their daughter to another. This gives the in-laws a right to torment the married woman's life.

I remember seeing a woman beaten up on the streets and people stopped and watched the whole episode laughing and not stopping it from happening. These people said this was a furore between husband and wife so they would not get involved. They believed that a husband had a right to discipline his own wife the way he wanted.

I do not blame such men. I blame the society they were raised in and the culture that perpetuates that kind of thinking. Some of the men are corky because they had a lot of money and cows taken away by the woman's family when they married her. However, there is no excuse for violence and abuse.

As for the parents who married their daughter away, they should learn to understand the consequences of their actions. Commodification of women is a big problem. They should not give a deaf ear to their children. They should break some of the cultural barriers that perpetuate the exploitation of women.

They might not have the guts to intervene when their child is being abused for fear of returning lobola, or dowry money. They might have spent the money, invested it into other projects or keeping it for their son or sons who can use it for education or to pay *lobola* to another family.

I understand that culture puts pressure to conform to certain norms. I understand this. I grew up in that era. My generation was a victim to these practices.

We are still a long way from changing these practices. I am aware of that, but why are we not making the effort? These backward practices are some of the very causes of abuse and violence. I do wish that my people and all the fathers who wish to give their daughters for marriage in future should always have love and care for their child and one of demonstrating that is not to charge too much money for *lobola*. They should charge fairly as a way of building a relationship. They should do it in a manner that their girl child would have a peaceful marriage.

I hope and pray that these people practising this way of 'selling' their child should stop at once and regard marriage as something special not a business transaction. What good or benefit does it bring to a family when you sell one member to buy another?

My generation perished because of promiscuity. There is the belief that most men are not satisfied by one woman. At the beginning of a marriage, it seems as if the relationship is a "match made in Heaven." The relationship changes after some time.

Most women have complained about being cheated on or being left soon after giving birth. At the time, they are going through the stresses and strains of breastfeeding and postnatal depression, men tend to look elsewhere for fun. That is the time they go out there to look for a much younger woman. Men from my generation always have the excuse that they do not want to hear a baby's cry, the smell of milk, and their wife being on a period. These are the excuses they give for abandoning a woman at their most vulnerable.

My eyes opened when I came to England and lived here for almost thirty years. For the first time I was surprised to see a man licking a woman's private parts and enjoying it. I had never seen this kind of pornography before. The man even got to the extent of sucking the woman's breast and feed from the same breasts that were feeding his child.

In a way, it is all right for as long as the two agree. I will not go that far for it is not part of my culture. However, in spite of what I think of this, it is an expression of love.

I wonder why in my culture men and women grow apart as soon as they get married. I have learnt that in order to keep the flame of love burning, couples should be in close contact with God. This would help to strengthen their relationship. I believe that charging less for *lobola* would also guarantee the safety of their girl child. It takes away the felling that 'I bought you, you're mine and I can do anything I want'.

I should stress that there are changes taking place now. While the norm was to charge a lot and not send the girl child to school, now things have changed. I thank God that the practice has been toned down. Most families in Africa are now educating their girl child and domestic violence and abuse have been reduced, but are to become outdated.

It is great that women are now a priority in families and a girl child is being treated as equally as the boy child is. We all had wished that move for our generation. It would make everyone equal in the family because everyone is bringing an income.

All parents out there should understand that education is the key. They should educate their girl child so that the struggle of having to stay in a marriage for financial gain would stop. Education is the key to a better life for everyone. It allows families to live happily and helps remove gender differences that exist in the world.

It is my belief that education also allows men and women to be at par and allows partners to be respectful of each other. In the end that would help marriages last. People would be marrying for love and not necessarily financial benefits. Women will have more choices if they are abused. They would be able to look after themselves outside of the marriage institution.

We should all embrace the changes of educating a girl child for it cuts the levels of domestic violence and abuse dramatically. It also educates men about their prejudices and their abuse. It should be stressed that men are making some headway in being aware that women have the same abilities as them. They have also become aware that there is nothing wrong with a woman having a career even if she has a child. Some men now help with roles that were traditionally said to be for women.

In the past, it was considered a woman's job to look after the kids, to cook and to carry out many other household chores. It is encouraging to realise that things have changed. We are not there 100 percent, but there is progress in putting a woman into a better position. Thank God for those changes. Although it took time, that is how life is like. Nothing stays permanent. However, we celebrate the changes to women's lives. The emancipation of women is progressing and we embrace the emerging culture.

TWENTY TWO

CAN THE SCARS OF DOMESTIC VIOLENCE GO?

Domestic violence is real. One can never get away from it, especially if you were as afraid as I was. Having grown up witnessing it in my own family, it did not do me any good at all. I thought that was normal and that is how marriages are. In retrospect, I can safely say that I had not seen a good example of marriage throughout my life. What I knew was that women should always submit to their husbands. In contrast, it was expected that husbands should always voice their opinions and give orders and women should keep their mouth shut. Under no circumstances should a wife answer back.

After the last husband had left, I felt relieved. Although I cried for days feeling sorry for myself, I had to come to terms with being single once more. I was happy, but at the same time confused and not sure I was going to survive in a society that only valued women in relation to their husbands.

I wanted to forgive and forget all my experiences. However, the reminder was the constant walking to the clinic for check-up and medication. The more tests they carried out on me, trying different medication to check for side effects, the more I remembered how these men had abused me. This made me very angry and unforgiving.

As it was my secret, I remained in the dark corner for many years and one can imagine what was going on in my head for those thirty years. I always knew I had to confront my ghosts. One way of doing this was to visit the places where I have lived with the men I now call my tormentors. I felt that this would make me forget about the experiences in the end. However, the first time I visited these places, I hated the move because all the painful experience came back. This was despite the fact that this was fifteen years later. I realised I was still hurting and going there to try to forgive made it worse.

The nightmares began once more even after counselling. Although I was in the United Kingdom and those people had since died, the situation did not get better. Working with counsellors, doctors and nurses helped me a lot. Members of my church were also supportive and encouraging. I had to learn to forgive myself first by not being hard on myself. The acceptance of my illness and the fact that my HIV check-up test result was showing that my viral load was undetectable helped me change my life.

Gradually, I started changing the way I saw things and became relaxed. When I was now able to discuss my illness without running tears, I then knew I had won the battle. I now started prayers and learnt how to forgive.

A lot of my friends and family could not believe the way I now handled my story. I could now talk to anyone and laugh about it. I had lived a long life and I could never be happier. Both husbands that had tormented me were now dead, the rapist and the abuser. I thank God for calling them at the time He did.

Although they did all this to me, I forgive them and may their souls rest in peace. I am now a new woman and I live my life for God. My faith has made me whole. My hope is that no girl child will ever suffer as I did just because of marriage. In addition, my other hope is that society will change and not impose the burden that it did on me.

Had I taken a quick decision to get myself out of this horrible situation, I would have been dead by now. My two late husbands knew very well that I was innocent, but they had to find manipulative ways of throwing it all to me.

This experience gave me a lot of wisdom and in my later years, I can now spot abuse better than before. If I talk to young girls, I can often tell if they are a victim of domestic abuse. I understand that this is a serious issue that needs to be taken seriously, but with the insight that I have, I feel I can see the telltale signs. Usually it takes long to spot people who are being abused or being controlled. It takes experience to spot the signs.

Young women want to believe that everything that happens to them is for love. Sometimes they go to the extent of blaming themselves for the behaviour of men. They try hard to change things or to win the love of a man whose heart is not there anymore.

My aim now is to help some of these young people to move from this mentality of self-blame. They should know that there is hope. I want young women to know that the scars of domestic abuse will not live with them forever. It is entirely up to the individual to choose to brush it under the carpet and pretend it never happened or to stand stall and confront it.

It took me thirty years of living a secret life and tormenting my own feelings. It was a long time of pain, and the torment shows in the health problems that I developed, for example HIV and high blood pressure.

I suffered and went through the torment. I could have gone out and preached to the whole world how men are like. No one would have blamed me. However, announcing my diagnosis and my pain to the world would not have helped my cause. In any case, I was constrained by culture and social expectations. Speaking out about my situation was an act of defiance. It was acting against my family and my society. Therefore, I had no courage to speak out anyway.

It was hurting me very badly to remain silent. I feared for my life and that of my child. I also worried about how my family would be viewed by the rest of society. I feared that I would be ostracised and no one would want to be close to me. This was the 1980s. My life would have been a 'living hell'.

The only way to save my child, my family and myself was to suffer in silence. I remained silent until I met people who could understand my position and my story. Those people made me see some light at the end of the tunnel. I went through counselling and joined groups of people who had suffered the same abuse and groups with HIV positive people. This gave me some hope. Seeing people who were living normal lives despite HIV diagnoses gave me some inspiration to continue with my life as normal.

I continued to attend those counselling sessions. They were very helpful. I was now able to deal with my situation better because I saw like-mined people and people I identified with. What I needed to understand was that the condition I had was now my new life. There was no reverse and my only choice now was to accept it. Healing starts with acceptance of the dilemma you face in life.

I was now able to nurse my heart and heal. The healing process became easier after accepting my condition as real. The decision to be happy was easier to make, knowing that my condition was not a death sentence and knowing that I had a support structure in place.

The scars, however, are permanent but what I choose to do with them is my decision. I decided not to keep reminding myself of the dark days by constantly crying, but to empower other women, especially the young and vulnerable ones.

Scars are indeed reminders of a storm, but they should not stop me from living a normal life. In order to live that life, I have to always take care of myself. I also have to be honest to my partner about my condition and my past if I choose to love again.

Remember once a storm comes and causes some damage, there will always be some scarring that will not disappear. There will always be a sign of that storm, but the repair work will be done. Therefore, while I have gone through the storm of abuse and illness, the reminder will always be those tablets I take every day. I might be looking healthy and beautiful, but that is because of God's favour. I consider myself as one of the chosen ones. Thank you Jesus!

TWENTY THREE

PEACE AFTER THE STORM

"A Psalm of David. The Lord is my shepherd; I shall not want. He makes me lie down in green pastures. He leads me beside still waters. He restores my soul. He leads me in paths of righteousness for his name's sake. Even though I walk through the valley of the shadow of death, I will fear no evil, for you are with me; your rod and your staff, they comfort me. You prepare a table before me in the presence of my enemies; you anoint my head with oil; my cup overflows. ..."
Psalm 23, Verse 1-6.

One has to make a choice and draw the line. Do you want to hurt all your life or you want to live a good life? After those good thirty years of emotionally pressurising my heart and my brain, I had to make a strong decision to die or not to die.

I then found it worthy to start healing to release myself from anger, hurt and deceit. I fought this war in silence, but I finally decided it was time to educate others and save lives. I felt that if I saved even just one life, I would have achieved my goal. I felt that if I did not do this, my people would die of lack of knowledge. If I was not going to help, my suffering and my pain would not have been worthy of anything.

I vowed not to be like my parents who believed in keeping abusive relationships a secret because they had been paid *lobola*. Those aunts and uncles who married me away had benefited by getting some money and they were determined to make sure that I stayed in the marriage, despite all the abuse that I got from it.

This culture of being 'everyone's child' should be abolished. I understand the idea that it takes a community to raise a child. Nevertheless, that maxim is not tantamount to abuse and infliction of pain on the child that is being raised. It is not a ticket to torment young women. Having a group of villagers decide on my life at my expense seems like a harsh and cruel act. It defeats the whole purpose of raising a child in a community where individuals and morals are respected.

Hope and prayer kept me going during my storm. In silence, I would cry myself a river and sleep. I turned my pillow when the tears had soaked one side wet. I cried myself to my sleep so that I could keep my marriage alive, for fear of being an outcast. Was there any marriage or love or was I was only a piece of meat?

I thank you Lord for the good years I struggled in turmoil. It was because of my ordeal that I became a resilient and strong woman. The wisdom I developed during my tribulations keeps me optimistic and hoping for a better tomorrow. It lifted the heavy load on my shoulders.

My goal is to set myself free and generations to come. By speaking and writing about my experience of domestic violence and domestic abuse, I hope, will save many people. I liberated myself and those emotions will never hound me again; but that is just part of the story. I now need to focus on others who may not be as lucky as I was to come out of such a situation.

I chose to be an author of domestic violence stories to save lives, not just from domestic violence and abuse, but also from HIV and AIDS. Contracting HIV during the storm will always be a reminder of the struggle and pain I went through and that memory will remain with me until I die. Although my CD4 count is high and my viral load is undetectable, there are moments of weakness and of sickness, making me uncomfortable. I have to remember always that my immune system is vulnerable and could easily be compromised. I should keep myself active and well.

Taking pills everyday has become part of my life. However, taking them for thirty years has had its own impact on me. I do ask myself always, "Am I normal or not?" The answer is, "Yes I am normal." Pills just slowdown my energy levels most times and some days are just unbearable.

TWENTY FOUR

TILL NEXT TIME

As we all know when the storm comes, it leaves no stone unturned. The ground shakes, the trees are left without leaves some of the houses were moved to different location and some actually destroyed and vanished. I had to be like a lion in its den and stood up to face the storm. What a challenge to my life?

God made sure he kept me alive so I can testify to the world. Who am I to say it just happened? It is not that I am cleverer than anyone else is. The favour of God kept me going. Looking back, I now come to believe that maybe the HIV diagnosis was a scare that made me realise that I was in an abusive relationship. An important event stopped me from sleepwalking into another marriage again. That freed me to do the work that I am doing now. There is nothing wrong, after all, in staying single. Being a single woman has so many advantages. I can do this important work without anyone making me feel worthless. Culture or no culture, I am still standing. I am happy. I am healthy. I am using my pain to inspire others.

While I realise the importance of cultural norms and practices, like those that accompany *lobola* payments, I also feel that they constrict progress and they perpetuate behaviours that promote abuse and exploitation of women and the girl child. I feel that these cultural practices are not right. They do not promote independence, creativity, love and family cohesion. In fact, they do the opposite. They promote family problems and are divisive. There is no love if love is based on commodification of women.

Traditionally and even today, *lobola* money in many families was taken to educate male members of the family and fund their leisure moments, but was meant to promote family cohesion, family ties and family progress. It was meant to bring two families together in a spirit of love, respect and understanding.

People may argue that this is Africa, and Africa has its own practices. That may be true, but human rights are indivisible. They are universal and all societies should be involved in their pursuit. While lobola traditionally was a way of making money, there are other means of living and there are other ways of making money.

I would never hurt my parents. It was cultural practices that put pressure on them. I think they could have thought about me as well. I guess my father could not do it alone as I mentioned before.

In Africa, I am not only my father's daughter, but also the whole village's. They say it takes a village to raise a child. It took a village to demand *lobola* too. As for my mother, I am sure inwardly she was hurting too, but she had no voice as not all women had a voice in such matters.

The situation now seems to be changing since the growing calls for the emancipation of women. Many changes have taken place in my native Zimbabwe since the early 1980s. I hope and pray that these changes will keep coming so that the value of a woman is recognised and respected. It is my sincere hope that these change brought in society will allow women not to be seen as chattels like pieces of furniture that are only there to decorate the household.

With God, all things are possible. I have come to understand my purpose in life much better. I also understand that I can be happy being single; but also that I am capable of forming good and lasting relationships. I have found a way to protect myself inwardly and outwardly and can confront whatever comes my way. I do not lose sleep over some of the things I used to worry about anymore.

I find comfort in the Bible and knowing who I am before Christ. He has given me my life back. Now I do not have nightmares of my future. I am excited about the future. Even though I do not have any physical relationship with anyone, I have a spiritual relationship with my father, Jesus Christ. I do not fear anything or anyone. I am a fighter and I fight a good fight. I receive anything that comes my way and I allow my Father to give me strength to win that fight.

Temptation is always there but the power of God restrains me from getting involved in things that could lead me back to where I am coming from. Thank you Lord. My life has shifted to the best side. I count myself lucky. My role now is to counsel young girls about life. I am a Life Coach and I have the love of life.

If I trace my life journey and the storm that I encountered along the way, I can safely say God saved me for a reason. I still have the support of my family. My father is still alive. Thank God for his life. He is in his mid-80s now. He too has transformed and understood some of the pressures that culture and society imposed on the family. He also found God and he is a devout Christian. He is also a blessing to my children.

I never remarried after all I went through. I never had any more children after my one and only child. My God has been so faithful to me. My daughter now has two girls of her own, my grandchildren whom I have adopted as mine. I am a blessed grandma and I love life. They say, "Make hay while the sun shines." Until the day I die, will continue to serve young men and women and save lives.

THE END

SIGN UP FOR THE JOSSINE ABRAHAMS
NEWSLETTER

If you loved **Peace After The Storm** and are already looking forward to the next great book from Jossine Abrahams, **Rise Above The Scars**, you can get the first chapter to read before anyone else...

For more details and to sign up for your exclusive chapter reveal head to:

JOSSINEABRAHAMS.COM

Printed in Poland
by Amazon Fulfillment
Poland Sp. z o.o., Wrocław